D1577623

STUDIES IN MODERN EUROPEAN
LITERATURE AND THOUGHT

General Editors:
ERICH HELLER
Professor of German
at Northwestern University
and
ANTHONY THORLBY
Professor of German
in the University College of Swansea

ROGER MARTIN DU GARD

Further Titles in Preparation

ROGER
MARTIN DU GARD

BY

ROBERT GIBSON

BOWES & BOWES
LONDON

First published in 1961 in the Series
Studies in Modern European Literature and Thought
by Bowes & Bowes Publishers Limited, London

Printed in Great Britain
by Richard Clay and Company Ltd,
Bungay, Suffolk

Contents

Martin du Gard was the most dedicated writer of his age. Like Flaubert, he chose to live his life in seclusion, fanatically devoted to his work. Throughout his long career, he steadfastly shunned the literary salon, the lecture platform, and the political arena. He contributed neither short stories nor criticism to literary reviews. Invited by Jean Paulhan to write for *La Nouvelle Revue Française* in the 1920's, he declined, saying: "Anything I have to say goes automatically into *Les Thibault*" (*O.C.*, II, p. 1107).* In spite of persistent pressure from many quarters, he refrained from making a single public pronouncement on any of the great issues of the post-war world, and spent the last eighteen years of his life, characteristically withdrawn, working on a vast novel which he never completed.

This lifetime of devotion to his writings did not go unrewarded: he won the Nobel Prize for Literature in 1937, his works were admitted into the Bibliothèque de la Pléiade in 1955, and were highly praised by such reputable judges as Rilke,

* Unless otherwise specified, references throughout are to the two-volume edition of Martin du Gard's *Œuvres Complètes*, published in 1955 in the Bibliothèque de la Pléiade, Gallimard.

Thibaudet, Gide, Schlumberger, Maurois, and Camus. But he has paid a price for his reticence, because by the great majority of critics his work has been consistently ignored. Beside the shelves of serried volumes devoted to any other novelist of comparable or even of manifestly inferior stature, can be set only two slim monographs,* two pamphlets,† a few unpublished University theses, and a handful of articles from literary reviews and manuals. If he was the most dedicated, he is also the least discussed of modern French writers.

This persistent lack of critical attention to Martin du Gard's work can only partly be attributed to his continual refusal to provide clues about his aims and motives. A more serious reason is likely to be that, however accomplished his work might have seemed to his own contemporaries, it is now considered to be as hopelessly dated as the poetry of another forgotten Nobel Prizewinner, Sully Prudhomme, and to belong to a tradition of novel-writing irretrievably outmoded by Proust. Martin du Gard would seem to have come to this conclusion himself: after completing *Les Thibault* in 1939, he grew more and more convinced that to the modern

* C. Borgal: *Roger Martin du Gard* ("Classiques du XXᵉ Siècle"), Editions Universitaires, Paris, 1957; J. Brenner: *Martin du Gard,* Gallimard, 1961.

† R. Lalou: *Roger Martin du Gard*, Gallimard, 1937, and H. C. Rice, *Roger Martin du Gard and The World of the Thibaults*, Viking Press, New York, 1941.

reading-public he was fated to seem like a relic from some vanished age. "The only place where I belong is the past," he wrote in his journal in 1943. "Whatever I think, whatever I say now will have no bearing on the questions that are being asked to-day and will be asked to-morrow by the young men who survive these present calamities" (*O.C.*, I, p. cxxi). In 1949, describing his lack of progress with his ambitious last novel, he wrote to Gide: "What I am writing at the moment seems to me incredibly out of date and to stand singularly little chance of interesting my contemporaries" (*O.C.*, I, p. cxxxviii).

The few noteworthy criticisms of Martin du Gard's work to appear since 1945 reveal agreement about his technical accomplishments but controversy over the survival-power of his themes. In 1950 at the end of her perspicacious and, on the whole, sympathetic study of *Les Thibault** Madame Claude-Edmonde Magny concluded with regret that "Martin du Gard's clock stopped in 1918". Yet in 1955 Albert Camus, whom nobody would accuse of wishing to escape into the past, ended a highly eulogistic essay on Martin du Gard by commending his work to the modern public and by hailing him as "our everlasting contemporary".†

* In *Histoire du Roman Français depuis 1918*, Vol. I, Editions du Seuil, Paris, 1950, pp. 314 ff.

† This essay prefaces the complete works of Martin du Gard in the Pléiade edition.

The object of this present brief exercise in exploration and evaluation is to determine if there are, in fact, any aspects of Martin du Gard's work that merit the attention of the present-day reader. It was inspired at the outset, and sustained throughout, by the conviction that though his exemplary devotion to literature ought not to be allowed to influence one's view of his actual achievement, it should at least entitle his work to more careful scrutiny than it has hitherto been accorded.

Thanks are due to Librarie Gallimard for kind permission to make use of copyright material.

I

The Making of a Writer

Those who fail in life are, for the most part, either those who take the wrong turning at the very outset, and wander off down a road not meant for them, or those who set off along the right road and are not able or willing to stay within their limits.

Antoine Thibault, (*O.C.*, II, p. 951).

(i)

There is far too little material yet available for a detailed biography of Martin du Gard to be attempted. Throughout his life, he remained quite inordinately reticent: his telephone number was only ever divulged to a handful of friends; during his visits to the annual symposia at Pontigny he resolutely refused to be drawn into the discussions. Only once in his life is he known to have addressed a public gathering, on 12th December 1937, when he had to make the speech of thanks traditionally demanded of Nobel Prizewinners. His friend, Louis Martin-Chauffier, reports that as soon as Martin du Gard learned he had won the Nobel Prize, he went into hiding, and that when he was accosted by Swedish journalists in the train on the way to receive his award he pretended they had mistaken him for someone else.* When, finally, he was pressed to give some account of himself at a press-conference in Stockholm, he firmly refused to discuss his private life, saying: "My friends know that I have what doctors call an organic intolerance for indiscretion. . . . A man who reveals to the public the best and most intimate part of himself through his writings, certainly has the *right* to be permitted to keep his private life to his closest relatives and to himself."†

The secrecy that surrounded Martin du Gard throughout his life has been preserved after his death. The last few months before he died were spent in classifying and packaging a great mass of unpublished papers, including the journal he kept from 1919 till 1949, and a great mass of manuscripts and letters; these were all deposited in the Bibliothèque Nationale and, on his instructions, will not be unsealed till at least twenty-five years from the date of his death. "Why bother to publish anything," he once said to a friend after the Second World War. "I can understand the urge to write—but this urge to *publish*! Publishing is the very opposite of writing." ‡

* L. Martin-Chauffier, article in *Femina-Illustration*, April 1956, pp. 97–101.

† Quoted by Professor Roger Froment in "Hommage à Roger Martin du Gard", *N.R.F.*, December 1958, p. 965.

‡ *Ibid.*, p. 1057.

Martin du Gard is known to have been an indefatigable letter-writer—the greatest of his time, claim some of his correspondents—but to date, only a handful of these letters have been made available. It is clear from these, from the brief descriptions of him to be found in Gide's journal, and from the various tributes paid him by friends after his death, that he was anything but the misanthropist his lifelong seclusion might suggest him to have been: he emerges as a profound pessimist, increasingly preoccupied with the thought of his inevitable death, yet deeply interested in his friends and in the vital public issues of the day, full of humour and humanity, capable of feeling and inspiring real affection.

When his journal and his letters at last become available it is possible that scholars will uncover deep-rooted personal reasons for his extraordinary reticence. At the present moment, however, for want of conclusive evidence, a simple explanation must suffice: like Mallarmé, and Proust, Martin du Gard considered his writing to be the most important thing in life, and he was much more resolute than they were in declining the rewards and the penalties of fame.

Though the secrets of his private life remained as jealously hidden as those of his close friend Gide were ostentatiously paraded, Martin du Gard did reveal before he died what he felt to have been the most important factors in his literary development. In the *Souvenirs*

Autobiographiques et Littéraires, which were first published in 1955 in the Pléiade edition of his complete works, Martin du Gard performed the remarkable feat of spotlighting the books and acquaintances who, in his view, most influenced him, and of effacing himself almost completely. In this way, he re-expressed his consistently held view that critics should concern themselves exclusively with his published work and leave his privacy undisturbed.

From Martin du Gard's *Souvenirs,* it appears that apart from the very important but incalculable effects of his professional middle-class home environment, there were three distinct sets of influences on his formative years: he was strongly tempted to become in turn a dramatist, a novelist, and a historian, and the story of his attempts to combine or reconcile these conflicting rôles is the story of his whole career.

Martin du Gard claimed, in all apparent seriousness, that his literary ambitions were first kindled at the age of nine or ten, with the desire to emulate one of his school friends, two years older than himself, who used to compose and declaim tragedies invariably set in Ancient Greece. This early attraction to play-writing was felt with increasing force during Martin du Gard's teens. While still a schoolboy, he became an assiduous theatregoer, paying regular visits first to the classical *matinées* at the Comédie-Française, then to the Théâtre-Libre when it was

14

making its name by presenting contemporary plays. The authors whose work the young Martin du Gard found particularly interesting were François de Curel, who specialized in the objective portrayal of problems of conscience, Georges de Porto-Riche, who preferred to analyse passion and the female heart, and Henri Bataille and Henry Bernstein, whose stock-in-trade was the psychological drama, heavy with violent and often morbid passion.

Martin du Gard considered that he would probably have begun his literary career as a dramatist had he not been decisively attracted to the novelist's vocation at the age of seventeen. During his middle teens, his father, alarmed by Martin du Gard's lack of progress at school, had arranged for him to stay with Louis Mellerio, a private tutor, who taught him that every piece of writing, from a book to a school essay, should be planned down to the last minute detail, and who encouraged him to study the construction of as many novels as he could lay hands on. Martin du Gard was never to forget these lessons, but though he would seem to have read through the French nineteenth-century masters with interest, they did not inspire him with any profound enthusiasm. He was not finally fired with the desire to write novels himself till he read *War and Peace*.

He was never afterwards to falter in his belief that this was the greatest novel ever written. Writing in the spring of 1916, to express his grief at the recent death of l'abbé Hébert, who had been his teacher and confessor at l'Ecole Fénelon and had first advised him to read *War and Peace*, he declared:

"I do not think I am exaggerating when I say that discovering Tolstoy was as important to me as some extraordinary *revelation*, and that it has had on my literary development, on my career as a novelist and, finally, on my whole work—I had almost said, on my whole life—the most decisive and durable of all influences" (*O.C.*, I, pp. 568–9).

Writing in September 1918 to a friend,* he hailed *War and Peace* as the greatest of all novels; he made a particular point of acknowledging his deep-felt debt to Tolstoy in the course of his Nobel Prizewinner's speech in Stockholm in 1937,† and in his *Souvenirs*, published in 1955, he reaffirmed that *War and Peace* had influenced him more profoundly than any other book, that he re-read it again and again, "always with the same fervour, always with the same delighted surprise" (*O.C.*, I, p. xlviii).

What Martin du Gard admired most in *War and Peace* was Tolstoy's ability to deduce character and motives through patient observation,

* Pierre Margaritis, to whom the whole of the Thibault chronicle is dedicated. Eight revealing letters from Martin du Gard to Margaritis were published in December 1958 in *La Nouvelle Revue Française* wholly dedicated to Martin du Gard.

† The text of this important speech appeared in *La Nouvelle Revue Française*, May 1959.

to portray unexceptional human beings with the very minimum of distortion, and to plan and create on a prodigious scale. These were qualities that Martin du Gard himself strove to emulate throughout his long career; he remained convinced that only by maintaining a lively interest in the world around him could he provide authentic data for his imagination to work on,* that only by employing a severely chastened impersonal style could he express genuine reality, and that only in composing a vast novel, with a host of characters and incidents, would he enjoy the satisfaction of stretching his faculties to their utmost.

Before he could embark on his career as a novelist, however, Martin du Gard's energies were temporarily diverted into a completely different channel. From 1899 till 1905, with an interruption for his period of compulsory military service, he studied history and medieval architecture at l'Ecole des Chartes. He took the entrance examination on impulse, with no prior

* Cf. "When I used to go out alone for a drink or to dine in a restaurant, by observing or listening to the person or the couple at the next table, there was scarcely an occasion when I did not pick up a whole host of hints: whether these were true or false is not important: what matters is to set the imagination working, to stuff your head with pictures, ideas, plots, then, when you come home, to record on paper a fresh and living note, which will serve as the starting-point for a book, or a simple episode, or perhaps merely a dramatic effect." Martin du Gard, letter to P. Margaritis, 6 February 1918, *loc. cit.*, pp. 1124–5.

enthusiasm for historical studies, but with the vague intention of developing his intellectual powers so as to enrich the novels he was still fully determined to write. When he emerged from l'Ecole des Chartes, however, he had not only acquired a certain amount of historical information and a palaeographer's diploma for his thesis on the ruins of the Norman Abbey at Jumièges, he had conceived a passionate interest in the study of history for its own sake, and abiding admiration for the scholarly diligence and integrity of his Chartist masters. Most important of all, he had become enthusiastically converted to the belief that thorough historical documentation is as important to the novelist as penetrating observation of the world around him.

Martin du Gard had been strongly attracted to the study of history, to the novel, and to the drama in turn because each promised him satisfaction for his particular intellectual and artistic needs. If he became a historian he could indulge to the full his passion for research: "I have a morbid desire to excavate, to go on digging into any problem till I reach bed-rock," he wrote to Pierre Margaritis in January 1918 (*loc. cit.*, p. 1123). If he became a novelist he could gratify his no less lively desire to build imaginary worlds of his own from the raw materials of his daily observation. If he became a dramatist he could still satisfy his urge to create, and by letting his characters reveal themselves through their words

18

and actions, avoid what for him were the acute problems of analysis: "As soon as I have to comment on a character," he noted in his journal in April 1943, "or analyse an emotion, I find myself in difficulties and can only extricate myself with considerable effort (Tolstoy's school, not Proust's)" (*O.C.*, I, p. cxvii).

For the rest of his career, Martin du Gard sought, with varying degrees of success, to remain faithful to the three great loves of his youth, to find a practical compromise between the wish to excavate truth from the vanished past and the wish to capture reality from the living present, between the wish to submit himself to the special limitations imposed by the theatre and the wish to range unfettered through space and time in a world as vast as Tolstoy's. His attempts to satisfy the conflicting demands of the historian, the novelist, and the dramatist in him determined both the content and the form of his work, just as on his ability to unite them all in a harmonious working-partnership depended its ultimate success.

(ii)

When he left l'Ecole des Chartes in 1905 Martin du Gard was still resolved to make his literary début as a novelist, but because he had yet to discover the true nature of his talents, and because, no doubt, he had till then viewed reality mainly through the prism of other men's writings, the beginning of his literary career was marked by considerable uncertainty both in his planning and his practice.

In his first novel, *Une Vie de Saint*, which he began to write in the summer of 1906, he set out to describe in minute detail the life of an imaginary village priest and the host of characters he encountered during the course of his long career. After eighteen months' hard work he had completed two volumes, and his hero had not even entered the seminary. Like Flaubert before him, he submitted his first novel to the judgment of a close friend: Gustave Valmont's verdict on *Une Vie de Saint* was as scathing as Louis Bouilhet's on the first version of *La Tentation de Saint-Antoine*. Like Flaubert, Martin du Gard accepted his friend's condemnation and abandoned his early novel; unlike Flaubert, he never returned to it.

The failure of *Une Vie de Saint* left Martin du Gard with the growing conviction that his confidence in his own literary ability might be misplaced. He had a wife and child to support by now and, though they were not suffering material hardship, he realized he could not afford to spend his whole life in abortive literary experiments. To exorcize his nagging fear of failure, he left Paris in the spring of 1909, moved into a hotel at Barbizon in the forest of Fontainebleau, and promptly set to work on a new novel, *Devenir!*, which was completed in a few months and published that same autumn.

Devenir! was dedicated to Jean de Tinan (1875–99), a minor Symbolist, whose introspective chief work, *Document sur l'Impuissance d'aimer* (1894), enjoyed a certain vogue with literary-minded young Frenchmen at the turn of the century. André Mazerelles, the unheroic hero of this first published novel of Martin du Gard's, illustrates the dangers of entertaining literary ambitions without self-knowledge and self-discipline: he never perceives his true potentialities or his true desires, and his life is a series of melancholy exercises in pastiche; he goes through the motions of being a budding man of letters, without ever producing a single work, and of being a great lover, without ever experiencing passion. The friends of his youth eventually make good in their various careers while Mazerelles grows increasingly lonely and dissatisfied; when at length he renounces his literary ambitions to marry and take up farming, he is merely copying one of his friends who seems to him the living proof that the secret of happiness is marriage to a farmer's daughter. But he is no more successful a farmer than he was a writer, and the novel ends with the death in premature childbirth of his wife and baby daughter, and his realization that he is hopelessly in debt and utterly alone.

Martin du Gard later dismissed *Devenir!* as a piece of juvenilia which he viewed with distaste and which he agreed to republish only with considerable reluctance. It provides ample evidence of the author's haste and inexperience: the hero's companions, who feature fairly prominently in the first two parts of the novel, disappear without comment in the third; his wife and child are summarily dispatched at the end of the book, not to express any Hardy-like pessimism or because of any organic dramatic necessity, but merely, one feels, because the author has tired of his therapeutic experiment and is impatient to have done; the hero's brief love-affair with Ketty Varine, a mysterious Russian adventuress, whom he meets and seduces in a hotel at Fontainebleau, and whom he hurriedly deserts when he suspects she may be pregnant, is distinctly novelettish in design and execution. The large number of subsidiary characters, Mazerelles' parents, the members of the literary group with whom he idles away his youth, the young *bien-pensant* set in which he tries to forget his loneliness, are all shrewdly observed and clearly distinguished, but they are a series of preliminary sketches rather than finished portraits. Mazerelles himself is well portrayed, for ever planning great victories in literature and love, and doomed to failure by his lack of resolution, but the average reader would find it difficult to read through *Devenir!* without tedium because the lack-lustre hero so dominates the book. Unless a *raté* is portrayed against an interesting background, like Frédéric Moreau in *L'Education Sentimentale*, or with some striking idiosyncrasies of style, like Meursault in *L'Etranger*, it would seem a self-defeating enterprise to make him the hero of a novel.

To the student of Martin du Gard, however, *Devenir!* is rich in interest because, like many another first novel, it contains errors of literary judgment the author will learn never to make again, as well as themes and situations he will treat again more masterfully in the works of his maturity. The insistence on self-knowledge as the foundation for all human achievement, the essential loneliness of the individual, the impossibility of real understanding between father and son, and between men and women, the diffident hero who shuns marital responsibility, the predatory heroine with a mysterious past, the contrast between the glittering expectations of youth and the dull reality of later life—all these are present in Martin du Gard's first novel and recur, in whole or part, throughout all his later writings.

Though most of the incidents in Mazerelles' life are probably not based on reality, one can see, with the advantages of hindsight, that the bulk of his literary projects are those of his creator: he is for ever planning ways to capture reality, "by the haphazard accumulation of facts and a spontaneous wealth of detail, to recreate Life" (*O.C.*, I, p. 125). He wants to "face Life squarely, to try to see it as it really is and not as other people have described it, and with what he sees, to create true literature" (*O.C.*, I, p. 126). He plans and abandons in rapid succession, a study of Montaigne and La Boétie, a volume of verse in the manner of Albert Samain, and a novel similar to *Les Déracinés* of Barrès, a work which may, in fact, have served as model for some of the group-discussions in the first parts of *Devenir!* itself. He is overwhelmed by Tolstoy and resolves to emulate him.

Mazerelles submits all his projects to the consideration of his best friend, Bernard Grosdidier, who, on Martin du Gard's admission in his *Souvenirs*, was fashioned in his own physical image: he is powerfully built; he is coached by a former *normalien* and then drifts into l'Ecole des Chartes; his pessimism and sardonic humour stamp him as a kindred spirit to Armand in *Un Taciturne* and the anonymous narrator in *Vieille France*, while his insistence on keeping well away from the Parisian social round suggests that he shared some of the temperamental as well as the bodily attributes of his creator; "I have one positive principle," he says to Mazerelles. "Produce literature by all means, but for God's sake, don't talk about it. At any rate, don't begin talking about it till you've created something, and gone on creating in a worthwhile way over a long period. . . ." (*O.C.*, I, p. 21). Mazerelles, with his grandiose ambitions, and Grosdidier, with his solid commonsense bordering on cynicism, express indestructible elements in Martin du Gard's own nature that were permanently in conflict. Out of this same conflict, he was to create the Thibault brothers; his inability to resolve it was probably one of the main reasons why he could never finish his last great novel, *Le Journal du Colonel Maumort*.

(iii)

However meretricious *Devenir!* came to seem to Martin du Gard himself, it won the approval of his friends when it first appeared, and performed the very necessary function of renewing his faith in his literary powers. With renewed confidence, inspired perhaps by his admiration for the works of George Eliot, he began work in 1909 on a new novel, *Marise*, the complete story of a woman's life, but he became so dissatisfied with his lack of progress that he soon gave up the project and destroyed all his preparatory work except for one episode. This he refashioned as a *nouvelle* which was published in 1909 under the title *L'une de nous*, but he quickly decided that this was far too mawkish and crude a work for his name to be associated with, and it was with considerable relief that he ordered his publisher to destroy the die and all existing stocks of the work in 1914.

In 1909 Martin du Gard was 28 years old and his literary career could scarcely have begun more ignominiously: two complete failures and one partial success with which he was already profoundly dissatisfied were all he had to show for years of extensive reading, diligent writing, and grandiose planning. The reasons for this most inauspicious beginning are not hard to find: *Une Vie de Saint* and *Marise* were subjects quite outside the range of his experience and his understanding. That a fledgling novelist who, on his own admission, was wholly devoid of religious sense or sympathy should have chosen to write at voluminous length about an imaginary country priest is only slightly more remarkable than his wish to describe in full psychological and physiological detail the seven ages of womanhood. One can only explain the choice of these uncongenial subjects as an extravagant precaution against involuntary self-revelation or as a perverse desire to grapple with difficulties for their own sake.

The imperfections of *Devenir!* can be accounted for, in part, by Martin du Gard's lack of planning and his haste in execution, but even more so by the fact that like Mazerelles himself, he was not, at this stage in his career, aware of his true gifts, and was thus not able to produce a work authentically his own. Only two of the three members of Martin du Gard's working partnership had been commissioned to write *Devenir!* The novelist had demonstrated his ability to observe and create character, but at the same time had shown a curious uncertainty in his invention of incident;

the dramatist had revealed his gifts for realistic and often lively dialogue, but the historian was wholly absent: apart from fleeting allusions to such period figures as President Loubet, Barrès, and Jean de Tinan, no attempt had been made to situate the characters in Time.

Yet Martin du Gard had already pointed the way to his literary salvation with certain of the plans enthusiastically conceived by his scapegoat, Mazerelles. Mazerelles plans to write a play or novel about a Catholic losing his faith; he dreams of writing a new form of book, half adventure-story and half social-novel: "he would take his place between Dumas *père* and Bourget; he would choose a historical subject and characters like the former, and, like the latter, analyse the delicate workings of conscience; he would bring individuals to life with the aid of documents and, with history to aid him, write a psychological novel" (*O.C.*, I, p. 89). Mazerelles, true to character, soon abandoned these projects; it was left to Martin du Gard himself to combine them and realize them in *Jean Barois*.

II

Jean Barois

The human community can sometimes help us in
our living, but can it help us in our dying?
> Albert Camus: *Roger Martin du Gard*
> (*O.C.*, I, p. xviii)

During his years at l'Ecole des Chartes, Martin du
Gard developed a passionate interest in contemporary ideological disputes and a scholarly
technique for studying them: "I am preoccupied
with all the great problems of the day, and I am
proud of the fact," he wrote to his friend Margaritis in January 1918. "I never stop working
in this direction or in building up my documentation; not a day passes when I do not take a note
on some philosophical or sociological question,
when I do not extract the essence from some book
on an abstract subject, when I do not cut out an
article from a review or a newspaper."* All this
material, he went on to say, was filed into classified
folders and stored away in the expectation that it
would one day serve his artistic purposes.

The question which seemed most crucial to all
thinking Frenchmen when Martin du Gard first

* *N.R.F.*, December 1958, p. 1117.

adopted this practice of copious note-taking, was the outcome of the bitter conflict being fought out in all fields of human activity between the champions of progressive reform and inflexible orthodoxy. The struggle was especially fierce and protracted over two particular issues: could traditional Christianity survive in the new scientific age? and should Captain Dreyfus, unjustly convicted on a trumped-up charge of high treason, be obliged to serve his sentence so as to maintain a façade of strength and unity in the Army and the State? Martin du Gard had not been personally involved in either of these controversies when they were first fought out: he painlessly shed his tenuous religious beliefs when he left his childhood behind, and never consciously yearned to regain them; while the passions roused by the Dreyfus Case were at their height he was still at school, and too concerned with clearing the next hurdle in his examinations to be tempted aside by political interests. In the first decade of the twentieth century, however, the battles of the 1890s were still being fought, not only in a great many books and articles but in the minds and hearts of a great many men. Martin du Gard made full use of both these sources of information: he collected a whole library of books on the Dreyfus Case, and studied them ten hours a day for six months;* he

* Martin du Gard gave these figures himself in a letter to P. Margaritis. *vide* N.R.F., December 1958, p. 1123.

collected as much evidence as he could on the bitter conflict between priests and free-thinkers, not only by extensive reading but also by observing its effect on his friends, such as l'abbé Hébert, who gave up the headship of l'Ecole Fénelon because he could no longer subscribe to Catholic dogma. Having amassed his material with the painstaking thoroughness of a trained historian, Martin du Gard then proceeded to fashion it into a novel. This was the way he approached *Jean Barois*, which made his reputation; *l'Eté 1914*, which won him his Nobel Prize; and *Le Journal du Colonel Maumort*, which was to have been a *Summa* of his lifetime's research and reflections. "First of all, I have to make a detailed abstract of all the newspapers and documents I have been able to lay hands on," he noted in his journal on 3rd October 1941. "Only when I have reconstructed the whole of the historical background will I really come to grips with my hero, and only then will the Novelist's task begin" (*O.C.*, I, p. cvi).

The writer who plans, like Martin du Gard, to build a novel from the raw material of authentic history sets himself particular problems: he must meet the challenge facing any novelist, must create living characters and impose his vision of reality on the reader in whatever way he chooses, but in addition he must organize his historical material to the best possible artistic advantage. He must decide first how much purely factual information can be dispensed with, how much is essential to illumine character and action, and then how best it can be imparted to the reader. He can choose to assume the rôle of Prologue and, like Scott or Balzac, set the scene in solid and minute detail and then retire to let his actors play their parts; or he can suddenly interrupt the action to deliver a history-lecture like Hugo in *Notre Dame de Paris* or Tolstoy in *War and Peace*. Martin du Gard did not adopt either of these methods in *Jean Barois*: the authentic controversies he studied so painstakingly were utilized not as decorative background but as the principal subject of the book; as Mazerelles had planned to do, he tried "to create fictitious characters out of his documentation", and "to write a psychological novel out of history".

Barois is brought up as a Catholic in a small provincial village. He eventually becomes a biology teacher at a Catholic boy's school in Paris and marries Cécile, a pious Catholic and a friend of the family since childhood. His inquiring, scientific mind leads him to ask questions that his religious friends cannot answer, and he abandons the Catholic faith. He resigns from his post, quarrels violently with his bigoted mother-in-law and his wife, and sets out alone to begin a new life in Paris. He makes friends with Marc-Elie Luce, the outstanding free-thinker of the day, becomes editor of *Le Semeur*, an anti-clerical, Socialist review, and, at the head of a group of Left Wing intellectuals, plays a prominent part in the Dreyfusard campaign. He builds up an international reputation with his books and articles hailing the triumph of Science over Religion, but shortly after lecturing a vast audience at the Trocadéro on the "Future of Disbelief", he is almost killed when his runaway cab collides with a tramcar: in the split second before the crash he involuntarily blurts out, " Hail, Mary, full of grace . . ." Appalled by this proof of weakness in his philosophical defences, he composes in convalescence a testament similar to that written by Renan at the end of his *Souvenirs d'Enfance et de Jeunesse*, in which he proclaims his belief in the infallibility of rationalism and disowns any words he might utter when he is weakened by sickness or old age. From then on, his materialistic faith is progressively undermined; by disillusionment with the cynical manner in which the Radical-Socialists exploit their victory over the Church after the Dreyfus campaign; by love for his eighteen-year-old daughter, who, in spite of all his rationalist arguments, remains unshakeably devout and becomes a nun; by fear of loneliness, which causes him to return to his wife after a separation of eighteen years; but most of all by dread of death, to which his reasoning can provide no antidote. He falls seriously ill, realizes he has only a short time to live, clutches at the hope of immortality held out by religion, and dies a Catholic.

When the publisher Bernard Grasset was offered *Jean Barois*, he refused it on the grounds that it was not a novel but a dossier; Gide, to whom the work was next sent for an opinion, advised Gallimard to publish it without delay, adding a comment that has been rather too often repeated: "The man who wrote this may not be an artist, but he certainly has power." Neither of these judgments is wholly fair, because each implies that *Jean Barois* is simply a heterogeneous collection of documents. In fact, it possesses the shape, proportion, and inevitability of a Greek tragedy.

The central theme of this drama is the hero's powerlessness to escape the effects of his heredity and his childhood environment. This would have been given greater prominence had Martin du Gard retained the title *S'affranchir?* which he originally chose for the novel, and which he later regretted discarding, but even without it, the progress and the significance of the action are abundantly clear. Like any Classical drama, *Jean Barois* is composed of *exposition*, *noeud*, and *dénouement*. During the *exposition*, the main characters are introduced, together with those fatal flaws in the hero's own nature that will cause his downfall: the bronchial weakness that will bring about his comparatively early death, and his fear of dying that will drive him back into the arms of the Church. His ultimate conversion is in fact prefigured in the fate of his father, who, after being a militant anti-clerical in the prime of life, becomes a Catholic on his death-bed.

During the central part of the novel, Barois seems to have successfully cast off the burden of his past. He campaigns fervently for Dreyfus not only in defence of justice but, as his friend Luce shrewdly observes, because it provides him with an ideal opportunity for asserting his independence from his early environment. Similarly, his impassioned rationalist crusade is not conducted purely for philosophical motives. It is when he seems to have detached himself most completely from his past that his past returns to claim him. Just after his long hubristic speech at the Trocadéro, calling upon his audience to cast off the shackles of dogma, his terror of death re-emerges, like the Commander's statue coming to Don Juan, to remind him of a rendezvous he is one day bound to keep.

"I believe in universal determinism," he declares in the testament he writes after his nearly fatal accident. "None of my actions is free . . . none of my responses could be other than it is" (O.C., I, p. 455). The vehemence of his materialistic pronouncements is dictated by his awareness of the power his past has to mould his future. "For a long time," he says to Luce five years later, "we picture life as a long straight road, the two ends of which lie beyond where the eye can reach, over the horizons behind and before us. But gradually we discover that the line is broken, that it is curving back, that the two ends are coming closer and closer together and are going to join. . . . The wheel is going to come full circle . . . I shall turn into an old man able only to go round in circles" (*O.C.*, I, p. 464). Barois sees his fate symbolized in Michelangelo's sculpture *The Heroic Captive*, a reproduction of which he keeps in his study.* Speaking to his confessor shortly before his death, he says of the *Captive*, "Look at him! He can't even get an arm free! Perhaps I've been just like him all these years, and only put on a show of being a free man" (*O.C.*, I, p. 538). A few months later, he dies in agony, reclaimed by the Church after his long, vain bid for intellectual freedom.

Far from being as shapeless as a dossier, therefore, *Jean Barois* has the neat logicality of a mathematical proof. It could, in fact, be argued that Martin du Gard shaped the work too deliberately in order to demonstrate the power of determinism. He eliminated from the life-story of Barois everything which did not have a direct bearing on the conflict he chose to portray. Just as in his own *Souvenirs Autobiographiques et*

* A photograph of this work was used as a frontispiece in the original edition of *Jean Barois*. L'abbé Hébert, to whom *Jean Barois* is dedicated, also exhibited a reproduction of Michelangelo's *Captive* in a prominent position in his study, according to Martin du Gard's own testimony (*v. O.C.*, I, p. 575).

Littéraires, Martin du Gard divulged only those experiences that affected his writings, so in *Jean Barois*, he included only those episodes which cast a light on his heroic spiritual development. The account of his childhood consists only of scenes anticipating his physical collapse in middle age and his death-bed conversion to Catholicism: it has none of that profusion of detail, included for its own sake, that makes *David Copperfield*, Tolstoy's *Childhood* and *Boyhood*, or Proust's *Combray* such rich and rewarding studies of childhood. His relationship with Cécile is observed at some length because it illuminates his spiritual dilemma. Because they provide no such illumination, his affairs with Huguette in his youth, and with Julia in maturity, are dismissed in a few lines. Thus, though it is not difficult to feel sympathy for Barois because of his intellectual integrity and for the warm humanity that informs his public actions, it is almost impossible to feel real affection for him because, far too often, he appears to be merely a disembodied mind.

The human interest which is the hall-mark of the authentic novel is not entirely lacking in *Jean Barois*: the scenes between the sceptical Barois and his childless wife, who is convinced that only their fervent prayers can at last enable her to conceive, the encounters between Barois and his daughter, and his final meetings with Luce, are the work of a novelist alive to the tragic elements in individual human lives. The dramatist's touch is also clearly evident: there are effective *coups de théâtre*, such as the arrival of the letter announcing the birth of a daughter to Barois while he is dictating a letter on the decline of religious faith, or the news of the suicide of Commandant Henry when the supporters of Dreyfus are about to give up hope; there are moments of dramatic irony, as when the young Barois cannot hear his father's words of materialist wisdom for the pealing of Church bells, or when the bigoted Catholic Cécile hopes that the materialistic arguments of Barois will dissuade their daughter from taking the veil and so rescue her from impending loneliness. But the contributions of the novelist and the dramatist to *Jean Barois* are completely overshadowed by those of the historian, who has insisted that large tracts of unadulterated ideological discussion be incorporated in the work so as to give each litigant as full and as fair a hearing as possible.

In the first part of *Jean Barois* the private drama of the fictitious hero is successfully integrated with the authentic nineteenth-century controversy over the relative merits of science and religion, although to clarify the issues at stake, Martin du Gard adopts the aesthetically questionable method of quoting verbatim or freely paraphrasing copious extracts from one of his source books, *Les Rapports de la Raison et de la Foi*, by Brunois. No code of laws, of course, exists to restrain a novelist from drawing on other men's work in this way, but one views it with a certain uneasiness, even when Martin du Gard, with characteristic integrity, is honest enough to supply footnote acknowledgments to the sources of his material. There would seem to be as little justification for borrowing *un-digested* extracts from a philosopher or a historian as for quoting with undue liberality from another novelist.

The second part of the novel largely consists of a reconstruction of the Dreyfus Case, seen from the viewpoint of Barois and his associates, who have first to be convinced by all the proofs of the innocence of Dreyfus before devoting their lives to his cause. The reconstruction is a model of its kind, so lucid, fair, comprehensive, and self-explanatory, that the summary of the *Affaire* by Jean-Bloch Michel, included in the Pléiade edition of Martin du Gard's works, seems largely superfluous. Martin du Gard's sources for his chapters on the *Affaire* will not be fully revealed till access is granted to his archives, but it is already clear that he drew heavily on Bernard Lazare's book *La Vérité sur l'Affaire Dreyfus,* and on the official transcript of the trial of Zola concerning the publication of Zola's famous open letter, *"J'accuse".* The reader's enjoyment of Martin du Gard's account of the Dreyfus Case is little impaired by his prior knowledge of its historical outcome: seen as it is, through the eyes of Barois, it has the same living qualities as the great battle-scenes in *War and Peace*. The chief critical objection is that during the prolonged campaign to establish the innocence of Dreyfus, the emotional and spiritual development of Barois is almost entirely lost sight of. He has a love-affair with Julia, a member of the *Semeur* group, but it is dismissed in a dozen lines while the Dreyfus Affair itself is allotted almost a hundred pages.

But if, in the second part of *Jean Barois*, the characters are submerged beneath the weight of historical data, in the third part they so dominate the action that political and social issues recede from the scene almost completely. While this is clearly necessary to allow the reader an unimpeded view of the steps leading to the reconversion of Barois to Catholicism, it is scarcely consistent with what has gone before. Neither Barois nor his friends are portrayed as senile dotards, yet they are suddenly bereft of their lifelong interest in the great public issues of their day, and make no comment on political developments in France and abroad or, even more surprisingly, on the philosophy of Bergson, whose books and public lectures had already begun to exert their considerable influence during the maturity of Barois, and provided a solution to many who, like Barois, found they could not reconcile the demands of their reason with their need for faith.

Martin du Gard's inability to integrate the

fictitious drama of Barois into the reality of history is most clearly revealed in his treatment of time. In the first part of the novel events are often dated: thus, it is expressly stated that Barois is twelve years old when the action begins in 1878, and the letter he sends a few months after his daughter is born, announcing his intention of joining the staff of *Le Semeur*, is dated 20th May 1895. Events in the second part of the novel, devoted as it is to the Dreyfus Case, are dated with extreme precision, because they are in fact authentic. In contrast, the time-scale of the third part of the novel is curiously uncertain: precise dates are replaced with such vague references as "A few years later" or "some months afterwards", and chronological confusion is worse confounded by the characters themselves, who all seem to be consulting different calendars. Marie Barois comes to spend several months with her father a few months after her eighteenth birthday, which, calculating from the precise data supplied at the beginning of the novel, means that the year can only be 1913. But during her stay, Barois, who was born in 1866, reflects that he is past fifty, which suggests that the year must be at least 1916. *Two years after* this, Luce praises Barois for his fifteen years of devoted service to *Le Semeur*, which indicates that the time is only 1910. It is odd that an author who always prided himself on his meticulous planning should have omitted to check his arithmetic.

Martin du Gard, who also prided himself on his impartiality, made every effort in *Jean Barois* to achieve complete objectivity: his Catholic characters, the mother-in-law, wife, and daughter of Barois, as well as the priests who seek to combat his scepticism, are presented with every semblance of fairness; they are all distinctive though mostly insubstantial personalities, none is a caricature; the free-thinking contributors to *Le Semeur* are not allowed a monopoly of the virtues, for beside the humane and tolerant figures of Barois and Luce must be set the intransigent sectarians, Breil-Zoeger and Dalier, who are as bigoted in their materialism as any of the priests ranged against them in their Catholicism. In every disputation Martin du Gard tries to present the viewpoint of each side without distortion or extraneous comment: the priests are allowed as fair a hearing as their rationalist opponents, the Nationalist viewpoint is represented as well as the Dreyfusards'. Each faction has its extremists and moderates. Each has also its one exemplary representative, Luce, the serene humanistic sage, and Marie Barois, no less serene in her piety; and between these two, painfully aware of the attraction of both views of life, oscillates the tormented figure of Barois, representative of a whole generation.

Martin du Gard, it might seem, has simply marshalled all the available evidence and left the jury of readers to arrive at their own conclusion, but he himself is not impartial, and it is not difficult to deduce where his sympathies lie. Those who speak for humanism dominate the book, not simply because of their vast intellectual superiority over the feeble-minded collection of priests chosen to defend the Catholic viewpoint,* but because the greater part of the book is devoted to the formulation and exposition of humanist views. Thus the materialistic testament of Barois is seen in full when it is first written, and extracts from it are reprinted at the end of the book, when his confessor discovers it after his death. His recantation is never seen directly and only fleetingly spoken of. Final victory in the struggle for the mind of Barois is won by the Church, but this is presented in such a light by Martin du Gard as to seem worthless and, with the furtive destruction of his last testament, more than a little ignoble. This impression is heightened by the deliberate juxtaposition of the deaths of Barois and Marc-Elie Luce: it is at once the most effective and the most revealing of the several dramatic ironies in the novel that Barois, who is reconverted to Catholicism

---

* According to later Catholic observers, this is an accurate enough assessment of the distribution of intellectual gifts between the opposing groups, at the turn of the century in France: *v.* P. Claudel, *Correspondance avec Francis Jammes et Gabriel Frizeau* (1897–1938), Gallimard, 1952, and C. Moeller, *Littérature du XXᵉ Siècle et Christianisme*, Vol. II, Castermann, 1953.

simply because of his dread of death, should, in the end, die hysterically. Luce, who has made an ideally happy marriage and produced a large family of devoted children, dies in agony after months of suffering, but remains stoically serene till the last, setting a humanist standard for his disciples and for Martin du Gard himself to aim at, in the manner of their living and the manner of their dying.

The form Martin du Gard adopted for *Jean Barois* had, like the central theme of the book, been earlier described by Mazerelles in *Devenir!* "I should begin with a description; then include a fact; next a character-analysis, another fact, a snatch of dialogue, a diary entry, a monologue, an extract from a letter, some more facts, more analyses. . . . Nothing but documents, in fact. I shall dispense with the watery narrative on which, in a conventional novel, all these fragments have to float . . ." (*O.C.*, I, p. 26). By thus dispensing with orthodox narrative, by concentrating on realistic dialogue, while describing the actions, gestures, and physical appearance of his characters with the greatest economy of means, Martin du Gard sought to take advantage both of the novelist's freedom to extend his action through space and time and the playwright's aptitude for singling out the most dramatic moments in the lives of his characters: events in his "dialogue novel", he hoped, would have almost the same physical reality for his readers as actions on the stage for spectators at a play.

Although, in his *Souvenirs*, Martin du Gard spoke of the dialogue novel as his "invention", works not unlike *Jean Barois* in form had already appeared some years previously: Edmond de Goncourt had employed a loose sequence of letters, impressions, diary-entries, and descriptions to portray the childhood and youth of the heroine of his novel *Chérie* (1884); *La Carrière* (1894), by Abel Hermant, and dialogue-episodes regularly appearing in *La Vie Parisienne* in the later 1890s were other examples, but were nothing more than light-hearted satires. Since the start of his career, Martin du Gard had been pre-occupied with the idea of making the dialogue-novel a serious and respectable art-form. *Une Vie de Saint* and *Marise* had both been planned as dialogue-novels; *Devenir!* had been composed as an orthodox linear narrative because it had been written at speed, and Martin du Gard had quickly discovered that the dialogue form set special technical problems that needed much time and ingenuity to solve. It was essential, for example, for the dialogue to be authentic and lively throughout, and to devise plausible reasons for his characters to be conversing together at a given time and a given place. It was necessary to distil the freely flowing narrative into a few quint-essential stage-directions.

In *Jean Barois* Martin du Gard finds a variety of

ingenious solutions to each of these problems: his sense of timing, his eye for the effective scene, and his ear for dialogue are all those of a skilled dramatist; he cleverly avoids undue monotony by allowing his characters to express themselves not only through conversations but by extracts from journals, interchanges of letters, newspaper-reports, or extracts from public lectures. It is by no means certain, however, that *Jean Barois* has in fact gained by being written in dialogue form. Martin du Gard was convinced that his cinematographic technique of highlighting significant detail and of quick cutting was particularly effective in capturing the rapid tempo of twentieth-century life. He reasoned that Society was in a state of flux and that the solid scene-setting of Balzac, like minutely detailed Realist painting, belonged essentially to a settled world. But quite apart from the fact that society in Balzac's day was actually in no less a state of ferment, even without the internal-combustion engine, one can dispute Martin du Gard's claim that his innovations gave *Jean Barois* greater reality. He held that his impressionistic technique enabled him to portray with more vividness than any other method would have done such scenes as that between Barois and his dying father or the riots after Zola's trial at Rennes; but on the evidence of *Germinal* and *L'Assommoir*, a much more convincing case could surely be made out for the claims of vigorous narrative as the best means of portraying mass movements.*

Martin du Gard's belief that his dialogues made his characters as real as stage actors was founded on a fallacy. If characters in a play have physical presence it is due to the living actors who personify them, not to the typographical lay-out of the script, which, in itself, is not necessarily more vivid and certainly no more "real" than a serious novel. The dialogue-novelist, in theory, enjoys the advantages of the novelist and the dramatist, but, in practice, at least if *Jean Barois* is typical, he is hampered by the limitations of both. Because he conceives his work as a play, he surrenders the novelist's unique privilege of being able to enter into the inner world of his characters, and he imposes on himself the considerable stylistic disadvantages of having to write entirely in the present tense. Because his work will never be staged, he denies himself the assistance of living players to enact his dialogues and so create that unique illusion of reality he particularly aspires to. The one great advantage of the dialogue-novel is its eminent suitability for recording abstract discussions, and the fact that *Jean Barois* is so successful an example of its kind adds conclusive weight to the view that what is of the greatest

*Martin du Gard's defence of the techniques he adopted in *Jean Barois* will be found in the letters to P. Margaritis, *loc. cit.*

importance in it are not the characters, but the ideas they express.

Even though *Jean Barois* was published in the same year as *Du Côté de Chez Swann*, *Le Grand Meaulnes*, Valery Larbaud's *Barnabooth*, Apollinaire's *Alcools*, and Péguy's *Ève*, it did not escape the attention of the readers of its day. But though Alain, Rémy de Gourmont, André Suarès, Péguy, Gide, and Paul Desjardins all gave it an appreciative welcome, it did not at once command a wide following. In the years immediately following, however, it began to command considerable admiration from many of the more discerning younger critics, writers like André Maurois, René Lalou, Jean Guéhenno, Paul Morand, and Philippe van Tieghem, who, in the volume of homage to Martin du Gard produced soon after his death by *La Nouvelle Revue Française*, all declared that *Jean Barois*, which had so impressed them in their youth, still retained their respect and their affection. What they particularly admired in *Jean Barois* is still worthy of admiration to-day: Martin du Gard's skill and honesty in so lucidly and so comprehensively portraying the great ideological issues in France at the turn of the century. It is extremely unlikely, however, that the young reader of to-day will identify himself so completely with Jean Barois as his counterparts readily did when the novel first appeared. The Dreyfus Case no longer arouses the partisan passions that once it did; the debate between religious believers and sceptics, though likely to prove unending, is no longer fought over the same ground as when Darwinism and Higher Criticism were new. In dealing as exclusively as it does, therefore, with issues that no longer seem crucial, *Jean Barois* has shared the fate of *Les Nourritures Terrestres*, which, quoting Sainte-Beuve in his *Notes sur André Gide*, Martin du Gard described as "one of those books that are 'useful', but whose life is short because the generations that profit by them are also the generations which exhaust them" (*O.C.*, II, p. 1396).

One's final judgment of *Jean Barois* depends on one's views of the function of the novelist. If it is held to be legitimate for him to deal primarily with ideological disputes, then *Jean Barois* is bound to be classed as a successful work, a full and reliable chronicle that can still be consulted with profit by all who wish to relive the controversies of a vanished age. But if the novelist's chief purpose is considered to be to examine the human heart and to study human relationships, then *Jean Barois* is at best a hybrid, the product of a very industrious but not wholly successful working partnership between novelist, dramatist, and historian, each resolved to reach truth by following a different route.

III

Les Thibault

I was still very young when I came across the
following remark about one of the characters in a
novel by Thomas Hardy. "The real value of life
seemed to him to be not its beauty but its tragic
quality." This corresponded to my own deeply ingrained beliefs which were closely bound up with
my sense of literary vocation. Already at that time
I believed what I still believe in to-day: that the
chief purpose of the novel is to express the tragic
aspects of life. I would add to-day: the tragic
aspects of the individual's search for self-fulfilment.

Martin du Gard, Nobel Prize Speech, 1937.

(i)

After *Jean Barois* was completed in the first
months of 1913 Martin du Gard gave his whole
attention to the theatre; in August 1913 he wrote
a peasant farce, *Le Testament du Père Leleu*, which
was successfully staged at the Vieux-Colombier
the following February; he struck up a particularly warm friendship with Jacques Copeau, and
in the last few months of peace worked beside
him each day at the Vieux-Colombier; he maintained his interest in the theatre while serving

with a motor transport unit during the First World War, and spent many of his leisure moments planning what he called his *Comédie des Tréteaux*, a new *Commedia dell' Arte* with a troupe of representative modern types always to be played by the same actors. Towards the end of the war, however, he began to think seriously again of his still unrealized ambition to become a major novelist, and during the first nine months of 1918 he several times discussed his literary aims and aspirations in an interchange of letters with his first cousin, Pierre Margaritis, a very promising musician, and one of Martin du Gard's closest friends since schooldays.

At the beginning of 1918 Martin du Gard considered that two quite different courses lay open to him: he could continue to take copious notes on contemporary abstract issues and produce more works like *Jean Barois*, or he could turn his attention instead to living people, and begin to write what he considered to be authentic novels, in which human interest would predominate.

On 1st September 1918 he wrote to tell Margaritis that he had at last made his choice: "My mind is made up. I am going to concentrate wholeheartedly on becoming a Novelist. I shall dispense with all philosophical theories, science and sociology. I am mutilating myself in the belief that I'm cutting away a carnivorous parasite that would have ended by devouring me.

Between what I can achieve by relying on my heart and my eyes, and what I can produce by raising myself up laboriously on my stacks of notes and on the books I'm endlessly annotating, there's as vast a difference as there is between a paper flower and natural blossom, or between a manufactured article and some living thing in its prime. *I am going to give all my time now to human beings*; instead of looking at books, I am going to look about me; I am going to run, to travel, to feel, to plunge into everything instead of shutting myself away in my library to cut out extracts from other books. In *Barois* there are far too many of these cuttings. I was stupid enough to want to cram into it all that I knew, all that I had picked up about religion and everything else." Yet for all that, he went on, he was convinced that certain parts of *Jean Barois* proved he had genuine creative gifts. "The day when I let these gifts grow to rich full bloom, without stifling them beneath the climbing weeds of ideology, I shall perhaps create works that will endure. The book that I am planning to write, that vast novel which, as I have already told you, is going to be called *Le Bien et le Mal*, I visualize as a pure novel, a story surging its way through many volumes, teeming with living characters, as arresting a spectacle as Life itself" (*loc. cit.*, pp. 1131–2).

In his *Souvenirs Littéraires* Martin du Gard makes no mention of this vast novel which, on the evidence of this letter, he seemed about to embark on in the autumn of 1918. Though his archives might reveal another *Jean Santeuil*, it seems unlikely, in view of his insistence on meticulous planning, that *Le Bien et le Mal* ever passed beyond the early preparatory stage, and it was probably either discarded altogether or transformed into *Les Thibault*. In his *Souvenirs* Martin du Gard declares that the seminal idea for *Les Thibault* first came to him in January 1920, when he was suddenly fired with the desire to write a novel about two brothers, "two people as different, as opposed in temperament as possible, yet profoundly marked by those deep-rooted similarities which are implanted in two people of the same stock by their dynamic common ancestry. Such a subject promised me rich rewards if I could split myself in two: I saw the possibility of being able to give simultaneous expression to two conflicting tendencies in my own nature: my instinctive need to escape, to rebel, to reject every sort of conformity, and the instinctive need for order, for moderation, for the avoidance of extreme courses which I owe to my heredity" (*O.C.*, I, p. lxxx).

Les Thibault, which Martin du Gard began to write in the autumn of 1920 and completed in the spring of 1939, describes the lives not only of two brothers but of the members of two families, the Catholic Thibaults and the Protestant Fontanins. The Thibault family is dominated by the father, an autocratic widower who has built up a public reputation for his good works, foremost among which is the reform-school for young delinquents he has founded at Crouy, near Compiègne. When his younger son Jacques is recaptured, after running away from school at the age of fourteen with his friend, Daniel de Fontanin, Monsieur Thibault has no hesitation in confining him in his reform-school in an effort to break his rebellious will. He is persuaded to allow him to return home only when he is confronted with the threat of public scandal that will jeopardize his chances of winning an important seat on the Catholic Institute in Paris. His life is dominated not only by his pride in his reputation but also by his fear of dying. When, at length, he is stricken with inoperable cancer, and finally realizes he is doomed, his terror is only assuaged by his confessor, l'abbé Vécard, who reminds him of the rewards he will surely lay up for himself in Heaven if he dies with dignity. But his resistance to death, first with the failing powers of his fear-crazed mind, then with the animal will to survive of his body, is so protracted, so futile, and so harrowing for his watching family, that his life has finally to be ended by an overdose of pain-killing drugs, administered by his elder son, Antoine, the doctor in charge of the case.

His death marks the beginning of the end of an era. During the funeral service at Crouy, Monsieur Thibault's surviving contemporaries assemble to pay him tribute. Without exception, they are decrepit, doddering, and moribund. Antoine surveys them with wry amusement: "They're all the same," he reflects, "they're quite interchangeable. Describe one and you've described them all. What a thin-blooded, rheumy-eyed, short-sighted lot! They're afraid of everything: afraid of new ideas, afraid of social change, afraid of everything that is beating against the walls of their fortress!" (*O.C.*, I, pp. 1360-1). His words have a prophetic ring of which he himself is oblivious, because the following year brings the outbreak of the First World War, which will destroy not only the crumbling bourgeois fortress but also both Jacques and himself.

Everything in Jacques Thibault's short life conspires to make him a lonely rebel and to drive him to an early death. Throughout his childhood he finds himself at odds with the authority of his father and his Catholic schoolteacher priests, and when these join forces to accuse him unjustly of forming an abnormal attachment for his great friend, Daniel de Fontanin, and, to break his will, imprison him in the reform-school, he is irrevocably alienated from the bourgeoisie and from the Catholic faith. He finds no happiness in love: his first, fumbling affair with Lisbeth, niece of the family concierge, is short-lived; he is always too inhibited to reveal his true feelings to Jenny de Fontanin, the great love of his life, and she always feels too intimidated to listen. After his literary ambitions have come to nought he finds, as Barois did, that Socialist crusading can allow him to forget his personal problems, but because of his middle-class background and his persistent refusal to countenance the use of violence in any form, he remains a solitary figure among his die-hard comrades. His desperate efforts to remould the world alternate with a no less desperate desire to escape from it completely. He twice makes an impulsive bid to break with his past; each time he is thwarted and plunged into utter despair: when he is brought back with Daniel in disgrace after trying to escape to North Africa he feels he is "helplessly caught up in the machinery of the Family, the Police and Society" (*O.C.*, I, p. 667). When, eight years later, Antoine runs him to earth in Switzerland, bringing the news that their father is dying, his immediate reaction is resentment at the intrusion into his self-imposed lonely exile. After he has visited his father's grave soon after the funeral, he reflects, as he has done on several occasions, that only death will provide the real solution to the problems of his tormented nature: "He longed to escape from it all. Not only from the clutches of society, not only from his family, from friendship and love, not only from himself, from the tyranny of heredity and habit—but to escape from the inner-most part of his nature, from that absurd will to survive which makes even the most shattered human body cling desperately to life. Once again, he was struck by the sheer logicality of the concept of suicide; disappearing completely of one's own free will, sinking at last into oblivion. He suddenly pictured his dead father and the beautifully peaceful expression on his face. *We shall find peace, Uncle Vanya . . . We shall find peace . . .*" (*O.C.*, I, p. 1368).

But Jacques is galvanized out of his melancholy brooding a few months later, in the summer of 1914, when a major European war begins to seem inevitable. While the extremists among his Socialist comrades, notably his embittered group-leader, Meynestrel, welcome the prospect of a great war as the ideal means of accelerating the collapse of capitalism, Jacques' profoundly humanitarian nature rebels at the likelihood of large-scale suffering, and he throws himself wholeheartedly into a campaign to save the peace. Ironically, it is only after he has found this cause for which he has been obscurely searching all his life that he and Jenny de Fontanin at last reveal their true feelings for one another. Their love mounts feverishly to its climax as, one by one, their Socialist comrades succumb to war hysteria. Jacques escapes to Switzerland, determined to continue his campaign for peace, to atone for his wasted life with one great heroic gesture.

Piloted by Meynestrel, who is in suicidal mood after being deserted by his mistress, Jacques plans to drop pacifist tracts over the French and German armies in Alsace. The venture ends in tragic fiasco: the plane crashes, the leaflets are destroyed before a single one can be dropped, and Meynestrel is blown to pieces. Though Jacques is grievously injured and bereft of his powers of speech, he clings to life with the same animal stubbornness as his father. He is picked up by a detachment of retreating French troops, assumed to be a German spy, and nicknamed "Fragil" because a splint bound to one of his fractured legs has been improvised from a packing-case inscribed with these letters. When the French troops are threatened with encirclement they panic, and Jacques is shot out of hand by a terrified soldier. His only epitaph is an obscene expletive, thrice shouted over his shattered body by his hysterical executioner.

Antoine Thibault seems at the outset to be the complete opposite of his younger brother: while Jacques is as clumsily idealistic as Tolstoy's Bezukhov, Antoine is as smugly self-satisfied as Homais or Monsieur Prudhomme. Love, death, social justice, and personal integrity, which continually torment Jacques, do not at first concern him in the slightest; as a competent and ambitious doctor, he is too preoccupied with medical problems to ponder over moral or political issues, and women are only permitted to enter his life to provide him with temporary diversion. But gradually he is forced to broaden his mental horizons; he is first jolted out of his complacency by a passionate love-affair with Rachel Goepfert, a sensual adventuress who assists him during the course of an emergency-operation, and who abruptly deserts him four months later; through being confronted with the problem of euthanasia, which he first encounters when he is asked to end the sufferings of a child dying of meningitis, and then, in much more acute and personal form, as he watches the protracted death-throes of his own father, he begins to search for the meaning of human life. After his father's death he lapses into his former habits: he is involved in an adulterous love-affair with Anne de Battaincourt, but finds himself unable to satisfy her voracious sexual demands. When war breaks out he goes to the Front without ever having considered the rights or wrongs of his country's cause, but simply to discharge the debt he feels he has contracted to the society that has provided his livelihood.

By the end of the war, little is left of Antoine's world: Rachel has died of yellow fever in Africa, Anne de Battaincourt has gone off to America with a new lover, his former colleagues have been killed or scattered by the war, while he himself, after being wounded and gassed, knows that he soon must die. To give some point to his few remaining months of life, he begins to keep a journal which he intends ultimately to be read by Jean-Paul, the son Jenny bore Jacques after their brief union on the very eve of war. He meditates on the problems of good and evil, and finds he cannot explain why he should have devoted his life to alleviating the pain of others when he has never believed in God. He surveys the outlook for mankind, and expresses his hopes that the League of Nations will prove a permanent safeguard against war. With equal detachment, he records the progress of the Allied counter-offensive in 1918 and the approach of his own death, which, like Marc-Elie Luce, he calmly accepts as an inevitable part of the natural order. Towards the end, his pain increases to such an extent that his diary becomes a mere case-book, in which he has only the strength to note the signs of his physical deterioration. The Armistice proclaimed on 1st November is not even recorded, and a week later, no longer willing to endure futile suffering, he ends his life, as he ended his father's, with an over-dose of drugs.

The remaining member of the Thibault circle is Gise, the Malagassie niece of Mademoiselle de Waize, who has acted as the children's nurse and family house-keeper after Madame Thibault died giving birth to Jacques. Gise, who is looked upon by Monsieur Thibault as a daughter, is emotionally involved with both his sons: Antoine at one time feels strongly attracted to her and even contemplates proposing to her after Rachel has deserted him; she herself falls desperately in love with Jacques, whose attitude to her remains that of an affectionate brother. She never marries, and shows her fidelity to Jacques by devoting herself to the upbringing of his son.

The Fontanins, whose destinies are inextricably linked with those of the Thibaults, have a less prominent but nevertheless important place in the novel. The father, Jérôme, is rarely at home because his life is largely spent in frenetic philandering. Though he always feels genuine remorse for his acts of infidelity, he can never resist sexual temptation. He retains a curious sense of loyalty both to his wife and his many victims: though he has lost all interest in Noémie Petit-Dutreuil, his wife's cousin and one of his numerous mistresses, he nurses her through a long illness till she dies an agonizing death in a squalid Amsterdam hotel; when he discovers that Noémie's former maid Rinette has borne him a child and become a prostitute he provides her with enough money to embark on a more respectable career and sends her home to Brittany, though not before seducing her once more. He finally shoots himself on the eve of the First World War after incurring unpayable debts through trying to keep two expensive mistresses.

Because of Jérôme's almost continuous absence, the Fontanin children are brought up by their mother, a Protestant clergyman's daughter. Though she rules by gentle example rather than by peremptory decree, her domination over her family is as complete as Monsieur Thibault's over his. Her own deeply ingrained puritanism is intensified by her resolve to prevent her children from following the shameful course of their father, but heredity and mischance combine to thwart all her efforts. During the course of his schoolboy escapade with Jacques, Daniel is sheltered and then seduced by a kind-hearted prostitute, and his life thereafter is given over to a campaign of sexual conquest. In more senses than one his exploits are predetermined by his father: he makes ineffectual advances to Nicole Petit-Dutreuil when she takes refuge with the Fontanins after her mother has run away with Jérôme; he pays successful court to Rinette, little knowing that what most attracts her is his resemblance to his father. His ultimate fate is as cruel as any meted out in the novel: during the war he is castrated by a shell-splinter, and the thought of the sexual adventures he can no longer have is made more bitter by the constant presence beside him of Nicole, the embodiment of all his unfulfilled desires.

When she is ten Jenny is stricken with cerebral fever and is saved from death only by the intercession of an old family friend, James Gregory, a Christian Science minister. This experience leads her mother to overstress both the weakness of the flesh and the powers of virtue, and turns Jenny into a neurotic prude. When she first senses the depth of Jacques' feelings for her she recoils in terror, and it is only four years afterwards, in an emotional atmosphere heightened by the suicide of her father and general war hysteria, that she can force herself first to listen and then clumsily

61

to respond to his protestations of love. Jacques' death genuinely grieves her, but creates for her a situation in which she finds perhaps the greatest happiness of which she is capable. When Jacques was alive she could scarcely bear him to touch her; now she devotes herself to the fervent cult of his memory and, in the military hospital run by her mother in the Thibault and Fontanin country houses that adjoin each other at Maisons-Lafitte, she expresses her defiance of her puritan conscience and her bourgeois upbringing, by flaunting her son's illegitimacy.

Great calamities have almost destroyed two generations of Thibaults and Fontanins; the old bourgeois order, both Catholic and Protestant, has been devastated and discredited; Jean-Paul, who represents a new generation and a new order, is left to realize the aspirations of both families. Antoine notes in his journal shortly before he dies: "All we hoped to do, all we should have liked to do, all we failed to do—all these things you must achieve, my child" (*O.C.*, II, p. 1008). The very last words in Antoine's Journal, scribbled after he has given himself the final, fatal injection, are "Jean-Paul", and so *Les Thibault* ends, like *Les Faux Monnayeurs*, with each central character thinking, albeit with different motives, of a little boy's future. The same interpretation could be placed on Martin du Gard's conclusion as Gide meant to imply by his: "Could be continued."

Though Les Thibault lacks the typographical eccentricity of *Jean Barois*, it reveals the same marked influence of the theatre. Information about the characters' past or inner life is supplied not by some impersonal third-person narrator but, almost invariably, through the writings or conversations of the characters themselves: thus Jacques' schoolboy diary describes the real motives for his first flight from home, while his short story, *La Sorellina*, suggests a likely explanation for the second; the story of Rachel's life emerges as she reminisces with Antoine over a film or a collection of photographs; the secret thoughts of Antoine and Monsieur Thibault are revealed in the private papers found after their death. Glimpses are permitted into the characters' consciousness, but for the most part they are portrayed through minutely composed dialogues, with every inflexion and gesture noted. "The one thing at which I am more or less proficient," Martin du Gard noted in his journal on 8th April 1943, "is at putting the reader in direct contact with the scene I am describing to him: to bring my characters to life, all I need do for the most part is to let them act and speak" (*O.C.*, I, p. cxvii).

He adopts a playwright's solutions to the problem of expressing the passage of time. *Les Thibault* can be seen as selected clusters of dramatic incidents, varying in duration, and separated by intervals of irregular length, during which the characters are transformed by events that are sometimes summarized in flashback, but never directly seen: in *Le Cahier Gris* Jacques is an impulsive young rebel, spirited enough to assert his own will against his father and his teachers; in *Le Pénitencier* he reappears nine months later so cowed that Antoine fears for his sanity; in *La Belle Saison*, five years afterwards, though still at odds with everybody around him, he has rediscovered his will to fight; by the time he appears again in *La Sorellina* three more years have elapsed, and his actions throughout the intervening period are simply listed in a single impressionistic paragraph; four years elapse between *L'Été 1914* and *Epilogue*, and during this period Antoine is wounded and gassed, completely loses his smug self-centredness, and develops a passionate interest in the great problems that confront all humanity. His experiences at the Front are summarized in a few brief diary-entries.

One disadvantage of applying this dramatist's technique to the novel is that Martin du Gard is not able to advance his several plots at the same uniform pace: Jacques disappears from the action after kissing Jenny's shadow on the moonlit wall in *La Belle Saison* and is not seen again till a volume and a half later in *La Sorellina*; Jenny makes her exit at the same time as Jacques and does not reappear till a third of the way through

L'Été 1914, nearly four volumes later. For the most part, however, Martin du Gard's sense of theatre proves wholly advantageous to *Les Thibault*, and it is nowhere exploited to better effect than in his narrative.

Martin du Gard's sense of timing enables him to meet the two requirements demanded of any story-teller: to arouse curiosity and to maintain suspense. This he does repeatedly by withholding the explanation of events till after they have made their dramatic impact: thus, the contents of Jacques' incriminating notebook are not divulged till the fury of his father and his schoolteachers has been fully described; and by permitting the action to be seen for so long strictly from the obtuse viewpoint of Antoine, he makes the reader share Antoine's uncertainty over the real attitude of Jacques' captors at Crouy, the secrets of the past lives of Rachel and Anne de Battaincourt, the true nature of the relationship between Jacques and Gise, and the reason for Daniel's unfathomable brooding after the War.

But the most distinctive features of *Les Thibault* owe little to Martin du Gard's interest in the theatre; they are the work of the "pure" novelist he had been intermittently striving to become ever since he first read *War and Peace*. It was Tolstoy who taught him to look for minute but all-revealing details, and to record them with the greatest possible clarity, and it is to

E   65

Martin du Gard's ability to put these lessons into effect that can be attributed the success of the most graphic scenes in *Les Thibault*: Antoine's operation on the severed femoral artery of the little girl, and the final parting between Antoine and Rachel in *La Belle Saison*, the harrowing description of the death-throes of Monsieur Thibault that takes up half of *La Mort du Père*, the final agonies of Jacques that fill the last long chapter of *L'Été 1914*.

The hall-mark of the "pure" novelist, however, in Martin du Gard's view, was not his ability to tell a story but his power to create character, and he considered that in this, it was again Tolstoy who was his supreme master. During the course of his Nobel Prizewinner's speech in Stockholm in 1937 he declared:

"The born novelist is characterized by his obsessive desire to penetrate ever more deeply into his knowledge of human beings, and to endow each of his characters with individual life, to reveal something in each of them that makes them quite unique. It seems to me that if the work of any novelist is to stand any chance of surviving, it will be solely due to the quantity and quality of the individual lives he has been able to portray. But this is not all. The novelist must also have a feeling for life in general; his work must be the expression of his own private view of the universe. In this, Tolstoy is again the supreme master. Each of his characters is more or less dimly haunted by metaphysical preoccupations, and each of the human experiences which he portrays can be seen not only as an examination of Man, but as an anxious search for the meaning of Life."*

Though only the main characters in *Les Thibault* can really be said to be "more or less dimly haunted by metaphysical preoccupations", they all have distinctive personalities, even when, like the patients who pass in melancholy procession through Antoine's consulting room in *La Consultation*, or like the Socialist revolutionaries who debate the international situation in *L'Été 1914*, they have only minor rôles to play. In his character-drawing Martin du Gard has deliberately tried to mirror life as it really is, rather than to present a highly coloured or magnified picture of it. His most important characters, unlike those of Balzac or Dickens, are neither wholly good nor wholly bad: the motives of Madame de Fontanin, who might seem to be a model of saintly long-suffering, are not always as altruistic as she herself believes; the documents found by Antoine after his father's death reveal that Monsieur Thibault was not the simple Pharisee that his words and actions suggested. Martin du Gard's guiding principle in writing *Les Thibault* as in *Jean Barois* was genuine realism rather than satire, and this is most clearly expressed in his portrayal of the bourgeoisie.

* *Loc. cit.*, pp. 958–9.

From the space he allows to outspoken indictments of the bourgeoisie in *Devenir!*, *Jean Barois*, and *Les Thibault*, it is clear that Martin du Gard was as conscious as any of his predecessors or contemporaries of the grave shortcomings of the *bien-pensant* middle classes: their complete lack of concern over social injustices, their uncritical acceptance of Right Wing and religious dogma fed to them since childhood, their over-riding concern for keeping up appearances; but, like Thomas Mann, he is realistic enough to admit that the bourgeoisie do not enjoy a monopoly of all the social vices. Though Monsieur Thibault's motives are mixed, though Jacques is as often filled with self-pity as Antoine is with self-satisfaction, they all devote their lives to the service of others. Similarly, though his sympathies clearly lie with the Socialist revolutionaries in *L'Eté 1914*, he remains fully aware that they can be as inflexible and inhuman as the bourgeois they seek to overthrow.

Not all of the characters in *Les Thibault* are fully rounded, however: Monsieur Chasles, the eccentric private secretary of Monsieur Thibault, is little more than a caricature, periodically brought into the action like a Shakespearean comic to introduce light relief after scenes of high dramatic tension; Hirsch, Rachel's former lover, who exerts such a daemonic hold over her, is never seen directly, but his crimes and vices are catalogued in lurid detail—he seems to have been imported from *Grand Guignol* simply to spirit Rachel out of the novel and to provide the unhappy ending to all human endeavours which is obligatory in Martin du Gard's world; Pastor Gregory, the Christian Scientist, is implausible from first to last, and shows the danger for a writer when he chooses a subject completely outside his range of experience.

Like most of his nineteenth-century French predecessors, Martin du Gard could involve his realistically composed characters in surprisingly unlikely situations. For all their much vaunted regard for observation and documentation, and their pretensions to realism, there are any number of incidents in the novels of Stendhal, Balzac, Edmond de Goncourt, and Zola, for example, which impose a severe strain on the reader's credulity. Most of the episodes in Rachel's past life are of this order: her first marriage to a sadistic opera singer who whips her regularly; her compulsive attachment to Hirsch, whose life-story reads like a précis of *The Romantic Agony*; the grave of her dead baby she occasionally visits in a lonely Norman cemetery—all of these might have been made plausible by the accumulation of minute detail during the description of them: because they are baldly reported, they temporarily reduce what is predominantly a realistic family chronicle to the level of a cheap novelette. There are other incidents in *Les Thibault* which are equally unconvincing for the same reason: Daniel de Fontanin breaking down the will of the reluctant Rinette simply by the magnetic power of his glance; the strong suspicions that before becoming Antoine's mis-. tress Anne de Battaincourt poisoned her first husband and formed a Lesbian attachment to her daughter's governess; Madame de Fontanin's being stricken with a mysterious illness at the precise moment when Daniel is gravely wounded on the field of battle. Some of these novelettish features, such as the character of Hirsch, who has much in common with Ménalque in *Les Nourritures Terrestres*, and the mysterious death of Rachel in equatorial Africa, which recalls the death of Lady Griffith in *Les Faux Monnayeurs*, might well be less-fortunate products of Martin du Gard's long and mutually beneficial friendship with Gide. The majority of them, however, like the more lurid lapses in the novels of Edmond de Goncourt and Zola, can in all probability be attributed to the imaginative heat generated from the clash between passionate impulses and compulsive shyness.

In a work the size of *Les Thibault*, however, these spasmodic excursions into melodrama are merely minor blemishes. What chiefly distinguishes the work, in fact, is Martin du Gard's perceptive observation of his main characters and of the wide range of relationships in which they are involved. Particularly impressive is his rich and full portrayal of the many aspects of adolescence: militant idealism, the determination never to compromise alternating with profound world-weariness, self-dramatization and self-pity, the whole process of erotic awakening, from the tormented *rêveries* of lonely puberty, through ethereal first love, to sexual initiation—nearly every twentieth-century French novelist of note, from Colette to Camus, has examined one or other of these adolescent traits in isolation: none has integrated them all so successfully into a single complex study as has Martin du Gard in the character of Jacques Thibault. Yet he is only one of several adolescents portrayed in *Les Thibault*: there are also the Fontanin children, Daniel, as greedy for sexual experience as Jenny is terrified of it, and Gise, who before experience transforms her into a frustrated old maid is, with her playfulness, seriousness, and capacity for unquestioning adoration, another Natasha Rostov.

The chief single source of the novel's strength, however, and, indeed, its *raison d'être*, is the complex of human relationships it portrays. Among modern French novels, only *A la Recherche du Temps Perdu* contains as intricate a range of relationships, yet though Proust probes more deeply than Martin du Gard, he also seriously narrows his range by his excessive preoccupation with male and female homosexuality.

Sexual anomalies are certainly not absent from *Les Thibault*: there is an equivocal element in the relationships between Gise and the Thibault brothers, between Rachel and her sadistic former lovers, and between Anne de Battaincourt and her daughter's governess, but the great majority of the relationships in the novel are normal. Heterosexual love is fully examined in all its many phases, from the tongue-tied adoration of the virgin adolescent to the bored satiety of the professional adulterer; and from the exultation that follows first possession to the despair left by final betrayal. Love, however, is traditionally the favourite topic of the French novelist, and it is the attention Martin du Gard devotes to a wide variety of other personal attachments that most distinguishes him from his contemporaries: filial love between Monsieur Thibault and between Madame de Fontanin and their children, fraternal affection between Antoine and Jacques, passionate friendship between Jacques and Daniel, mutual admiration between Antoine and Madame de Fontanin, genuine comradeship between Antoine and his medical colleagues and between Jacques and his fellow Socialists—no aspect of normal love or friendship is excluded.

Some of the human relationships in *Les Thibault* are studied at greater length and with greater subtlety than others, and one of the most noteworthy of these is the marriage between Jérôme and Thérèse de Fontanin. Madame de Fontanin persistently professes what she believes to be genuine loathing for physical love and for the obsessive lechery of her husband; yet, through a number of suggestive details, Martin du Gard reveals, without extraneous comment, how her puritanical horror of the flesh is nourished by her frustrated sensuality: she is profoundly moved at the sight of the plump shoulders of her cousin Noémie, whom she knows to be her husband's mistress, and deeply affected at the sight of Jenny and Jacques asleep on a couch in each other's arms; however often she may plan to divorce her husband for his repeated acts of infidelity, she can never make the final break, and it is only as she kneels by his death-bed that she realizes the all-powerful carnal attraction he has never ceased to exercise over her throughout their unhappy married life. Her deepest emotions are only ever stirred by the menfolk in her family, and the indulgence which she shows to her husband and her son, and which she involuntarily withholds from her daughter, accounts in no small measure for the contrasting attitudes her children adopt towards love.

In spite of the pronounced differences between the individual Thibaults, they are all recognizably members of the same family. Their most conspicuous common characteristic is their strength of will: in Monsieur Thibault this expresses itself as a compulsive urge to dominate, and in Jacques, as an obstinate refusal to compromise; in Antoine it takes the form of single-minded devotion to his career, and the supreme self-confidence which, in the end, causes him to neglect the most elementary precautions on the battlefield and so brings about his wantonly unnecessary death. From the few brief appearances Jean-Paul makes in *Epilogue* it is clear, from his mulish obstinacy and precocious wish to assert his independence, that he too has inherited the will of the Thibaults.

The love–hate relationship between Monsieur Thibault and Jacques is the most complex in the whole novel. They are inevitably opposed to one another because neither is prepared to submit to the inflexible will of the other; Monsieur Thibault's feelings are exacerbated by the reflection that Jacques is a child he never wanted and whose birth cost the life of his beloved wife; Jacques' bitterness is increased by the sight of the demonstrative affection his friend Daniel receives from his mother. Yet, despite the bitter recriminations they hurl at each other, Jacques and his father remain loyal and even affectionate towards each other, though their feelings are only ever revealed to a third party: Monsieur Thibault boasts of Jacques' academic achievements to the local tradespeople at Maisons-Lafitte, though to Jacques himself he gives little or no encouragement; Jacques hotly defends his father against insinuations by Daniel and Antoine even when, at his father's command, he has been sentenced to solitary confinement at the reform-school: in his father's presence, he is always either intimidated into silence or provoked into abuse.

When he returns from exile in Lausanne to keep watch by the bedside of his dying father, Jacques touches Monsieur Thibault's shoulder and is suddenly overcome with tenderness, just as Jean Barois is moved to pity when he kisses his dying father, to whom he showed no affection throughout his life. But Jacques does not feel compassion simply because it is his own father who is dying before his eyes:

"Suddenly the contact with M. Thibault's dank flesh stirred him, and provoked a wholly unexpected reaction in him: it was a physical response, a pure state of feeling far surpassing pity or affection; it was the egotistical tenderness of one human being for another" (*O.C.*, I, p. 1282).

This feeling of compassion, which both Jacques and Antoine come to feel for all humanity, is consistently expressed in Martin du Gard's treatment of character and situation throughout *Les Thibault*. It enables him to exploit to the full his "gift for seeing and expressing the commonplace dramas being played out in the hidden recesses of every human life",* which constitutes his chief claim to be considered as an important novelist, and the chief hope *Les Thibault* has of enduring.

* Martin du Gard, letter to P. Margaritis, 18th January 1918; *loc. cit.*, p. 1120.

The majority of critics who have written of *Les Thibault* have found its texture uneven and its structure faulty: "No one can declare that the later volumes are comparable to the early ones," Mr Martin Turnell has recently declared,* while even a commentator as sympathetically disposed to *Les Thibault* as Madame Magny finds there is more to blame than praise in the last two volumes. The burden of these criticisms is that with *L'Eté 1914* the character of the novel changes completely: what has been a family chronicle becomes an investigation into the causes of the First World War, the imaginary characters are engulfed in a flood of discussion about real events, and the result, like *Jean Barois*, is a hybrid unacceptable either to historical scholar or literary critic.

It was for many years an open secret that Martin du Gard did in fact radically alter his original plan for *Les Thibault* after it was only one-third completed, but not until 1955, with the publication of his *Souvenirs littéraires*, did he explain his aims and motives. On New Year's Day 1931 he was involved in a serious car-crash and immobilized in hospital for several months. During this period, after meditating on the first seven volumes he had written and the fifteen or more that were still required to complete the

* In *The Art of French Fiction*, Hamish Hamilton, 1959, p. 294.

project, he came to the conclusion that if he adhered to the original plan drawn up in 1920 he could not fail to destroy the unity of the work; merely to eliminate whole episodes and characters would, he felt, destroy the intricate web of human relationships he had been so patiently spinning. So he decided that the only feasible solution was to plan an entirely new *dénouement* and graft it as smoothly as possible on to the existing body of the work. To put an end to possible future prevarication, he destroyed all his preparatory work, including *L'Appareillage*, which was to have been the seventh volume in the cycle, and which, after two years' work, was almost ready for the printer. Five more years were to elapse before he was to finish the completely new seventh instalment in the Thibault serial, and nine years in all before he at last concluded it.

Though, in his *Souvenirs*, Martin du Gard briefly describes a few of the episodes he sacrificed when he burnt his papers in the spring of 1931, it would be vain to spend much time speculating on what *Les Thibault* might have been. Had he seen fit to follow his original plan, the likelihood is that the final result would have been a novel as vast and as invertebrate as *Les Hommes de Bonne Volonté*. What can and must be decided is how far Martin du Gard succeeded in imposing uniformity of texture and unity of structure on *Les Thibault* as it now stands.

Les Thibault was never planned, like *Ulysses* or *A la Recherche du Temps Perdu*, as a single vast edifice. It is made up of a series of novels, each of which covers a different period of time, and each of which portrays one or more of the protagonists at a moment of crisis and decision. The individual volumes of which the cycle is composed exhibit important differences both in form and content, and each may be viewed as the solution to a distinct technical problem: thus *La Belle Saison*, which covers a period of four months, is a quartet of interwoven love-stories; *La Consultation*, which is wholly devoted to twenty-four hours in the life of Antoine, is composed of dramatized scenes from a doctor's case-book, while *La Sorellina*, which intensifies and then explains the mystery surrounding Jacques' second disappearance, is a story within a story. "With each new subject," as Robert Louis Stevenson once observed, "the true artist will vary his method and change the point of his attack."*

Certain of the important differences between *L'Eté 1914* and the six preceding volumes may be directly attributed to the change in the viewpoint from which events are seen. In all the earlier volumes, even in *Le Pénitencier* and *La Sorellina*, in which Jacques is the principal subject, the action is seen almost exclusively from Antoine's point of view: *L'Eté 1914*, in which

* In *A Humble Remonstrance* (1884), reprinted in *Memories and Portraits* (1887).

events are seen predominantly through Jacques' eyes, is itself almost as long as the six volumes which precede it, because Martin du Gard has sought to redress the balance between his two protagonists. Discussion of abstract issues is not entirely missing from the earlier volumes, because with the growth of Antoine's ethical consciousness he begins to search for a philosophy by which to live; accordingly, *La Mort du Père* concludes with a long discussion between Antoine and l'abbé Vécard which reviews again the arguments for and against religion previously examined in *Jean Barois*. But Antoine is too preoccupied with his medical research to take more than a passing interest in metaphysics or affairs of state. This does not altogether excuse Martin du Gard for failing to date the early volumes in what purports to be a realistic family chronicle,* but it provides a valid reason for the lack of attention paid to the national or international scene. In *La Belle Saison* there is a passing

* Bernard Crémieux quickly drew Martin du Gard's attention to this oversight in his review of *Le Cahier Gris* in *La Nouvelle Revue Française* in May 1922. Even so, no specific dates are mentioned in *Les Thibault* till *La Sorellina*, which describes Antoine's activities on 13 October 1913. Only after deductions have been made from the precise chronological data supplied in the first two volumes, however, is one able to calculate that events in *Le Cahier Gris* took place in 1904, while *La Belle Saison* is set in 1910. Martin du Gard's arithmetic is on this occasion infallible, but it is something of a blemish that the reader should be obliged to hunt for data before he can check it.

reference in a newsreel to the Army's summer manœuvres, while Antoine is making love to Rachel in a cinema; and in *La Consultation*, Rumelles, who holds a high diplomatic post, tells Antoine of the growing danger of war, but Antoine shows no interest and, in this, he is reacting in consistent accord with his politically apathetic character.

Events in *L'Eté 1914* are mainly seen not from the viewpoint of Antoine, who remains immersed in his private pursuits till the outbreak of war, but through the consciousness of Jacques, who is a fervent Socialist pacifist, hungry for every scrap of news about the worsening international situation, and eager to marshal every argument at his disposal to convince everyone of the follies of war. If one concedes to Martin du Gard his right to change viewpoints in a novel that has two heroes, one cannot fairly complain if, with the introduction of a new protagonist, style and treatment change too. It is perfectly fitting for the reader to feel a change in atmosphere as he takes up *L'Eté 1914* after *La Mort du Père*, because he is entering a quite different world.

But while agreeing that it is perfectly plausible for Jacques to be so wholeheartedly committed to the campaign to preserve the peace, Martin du Gard's detractors can argue, with some justification, that it is by no means artistically necessary for every discussion to be reported in such copious detail. Martin du Gard's documentation for *L'Eté 1914* was every bit as massive and as painstaking as it was for *Jean Barois*, and on several occasions, as in *Jean Barois*, the novelist, who should have the right to select only what is relevant to his purpose, is overwhelmed by the historian, who is determined to include every minute piece of information which might contribute to his scholarly reconstruction. In the midst of a particularly long exposé of French foreign policy which adds nothing vital to the reader's knowledge of his characters, Martin du Gard seems to be trying to disarm possible criticism when he makes Jacques say to Antoine: "It's just as though I were giving you a lecture: this is ridiculous!" (*O.C.*, II, p. 137). In his *Souvenirs* he admits that because of his Chartist training he attached probably excessive importance to the virtues of documentation: "The joke is that while I was flattering myself that I was giving solidity to my works—I was possibly only making them ponderous" (*O.C.*, I, p. li).

Although there are several occasions in *L'Eté 1914* when one feels that Martin du Gard could profitably have condensed or even suppressed some of the ideological discussions, the personal dramas of his characters are not submerged beneath historical events as they are throughout the duration of the Dreyfus Case in *Jean Barois*: for the most part, in fact, the fictitious and factual elements are co-ordinated with the maximum of dramatic effect. Like *Jean Barois*, *L'Eté 1914* is

F   81

shaped in the form of a classical tragedy. The first twelve chapters constitute the *exposition*: they set the European scene in July 1914, reveal Jacques' troubled loneliness, his passionate humanity, and the birth of his desperate resolve to save the world in spite of itself. The vast and complicated *nœud* of the drama occupies sixty-eight chapters in which a day-by-day, often hour-by-hour progress report on events leading up to the outbreak of war is interwoven not only with the love affair between Jacques and Jenny but also with the affairs between Antoine and Anne, and between Meynestrel and Alfreda. The fact that the reader knows that the First World War will not be averted, in spite of all Jacques' efforts and all Jenny's hopes, adds real poignancy to their few brief moments of first and last love, which are in turn contrasted with Antoine's self-disgust and Meynestrel's despair. The last five chapters provide the *dénouement*, with Jacques' final bid for peace and his brutal death. Viewed either as a scholarly reconstruction of the atmosphere in Paris on the eve of war or as a moving human drama, *L'Eté 1914* is a magnificent *tour de force*, and must be ranked as one of the most impressive historical novels in the French language. The novelist, the dramatist, and the historian in Martin du Gard, for the first and last time, worked together in almost complete harmony, and the success of their joint efforts illustrates the truth of Flaubert's axiom that "the secret of a masterpiece lies in the compatibility of the subject and the author's temperament".*

Although Martin du Gard was first prompted to scrap the original plan of *Les Thibault* because of strictly formal considerations, the new plan he devised was shaped by a powerful factor that had nothing to do with form or style; his passionate hatred of war. When he drew up his original blueprint for *Les Thibault* in 1920, it seemed that the last war in history had just been fought, and he planned to trace the adventures of Antoine and Jean-Paul far into the indefinite future. By the middle 1930s, when he was fashioning a completely new *dénouement*, it was becoming increasingly obvious that the nations of Europe would soon be at war again. Martin du Gard's reaction was to give the First World War a much more important rôle than it conceivably could have had in the original scheme: what would, in all likelihood, have been a dramatic highlight in the course of a prolix narrative, becomes the *diabolus ex machina* of a much more compact tragedy, striking down both protagonists and leaving the world in ruins. This not only greatly increases the tragic impact of *Les Thibault* as a whole, it introduces an unmistakably didactic element that is missing in all the earlier volumes.

In *L'Été 1914* this is most forcibly expressed not through the pacifist arguments of Jacques and his comrades, which, as in *Jean Barois*, are

* Letter to Madame Roger des Genettes, 1861.

always met by the counter-arguments of their opponents, but in the brutality of the *dénouement*. Jacques' death at the outbreak of war was planned as early as 1920 and, from the very opening scene of *Le Cahier Gris*, he is led towards it as inexorably as Oedipus to his incestuous marriage bed. But if his death itself is dramatically inevitable, the manner of his dying is not. In a special version of Jacques Thibault's life prepared in 1946 as a story for younger readers, Martin du Gard chose to let him die as cleanly as Lauro de Bosis, the young Italian poet whose anti-Fascist leaflet flight over Rome on 3rd October 1931 was probably the model for Jacques' last mission. Martin du Gard's decision to make Jacques die so cruelly when he wrote the ending to *L'Eté 1914* in the spring of 1936 is an expression not of his sadism but of his anger at the spectacle of human folly and forgetfulness. "How gratified I should be," he said of *L'Eté 1914* during his Nobel Prize-winner's speech in 1937, "if I could believe that this work which you have honoured in my name could serve not only the cause of literature but also the cause of peace!"

Martin du Gard's deep personal feelings admirably served his artistic purposes in *L'Eté 1914*, because they lent credibility and conviction to the views and the destiny of the central character. Personal feelings played no less vital a rôle in shaping the last volume of *Les Thibault*, but with rather less fortunate results. By the late thirties, when Martin du Gard was composing *Epilogue*, it had become obvious that war was inevitable, and his fervent pacifism turned to bleak despair. He lost the urgent sense of purpose which sustained him in the vast labours of documentation required for *L'Eté 1914*, and found himself longing to be free again to write purely psychological novels.

Because Jean-Paul survives to carry on the hopes of the Thibaults and the Fontanins and because Antoine refuses to surrender to complete despair, the more enthusiastic of Martin du Gard's supporters have hailed *Epilogue* as an admirable hymn to life. It is difficult for a more detached observer to view it as anything but the work of a bewildered and disillusioned author who has grown tired of his characters and is impatient to have done with them. Martin du Gard's fatigue is apparent both in the form and the content of *Epilogue*: in the events that bring about Antoine's death which are perfectly plausible in themselves, but lack almost all semblance of dramatic inevitability; in the number of times Martin du Gard intervenes to provide rapid flashbacks of past events, thereby freeing himself from the obligation of devising ways and means for his characters to supply all such information themselves, as they consistently do throughout the seven earlier volumes; and in filling the last third of the volume with Antoine's journal, the literary form which, if he so wishes, can set the novelist the fewest number of technical problems. "I remember that I took no time at all to write Monsieur Thibault's *Posthumous Papers* and Antoine's *Journal*," Martin du Gard wrote to Gide in February 1945. "Why? Because over a long period beforehand, I had built up haphazardly a large store of notes and fragments which were able to serve my purposes. These parts of the book more or less wrote themselves" (*O.C.*, I, p. cxxiv).

Like Henry Céard's Naturalist novel *Une Belle Journée*, Antoine's journal demonstrates how dull a work is bound to result when an author sets out to mirror humdrum reality without in any way illuminating it. All of Antoine's observations are meticulously consistent with his somewhat drab character and his limited mental outlook: his thoughts are never more than trite, thus confirming the accuracy of his own assessment of himself as a commonplace person with little understanding of himself, or of the world about him; his medical notes on his bronchial deterioration and the occasional references he makes to the towns and villages recaptured during the Allied counter-offensive of 1918 are now virtually incomprehensible without explanatory footnotes, and even with these no further insight would be gained into Antoine's character. As for the fervent hopes repeatedly voiced in the policies of President Wilson and in the League of Nations, these realistically reflect an optimism that was widely shared in 1918, but considered as the work of a novelist writing in 1938, they must be looked upon as an expression of the author's irony or his escapism. From the late thirties, in fact, can be dated Martin du Gard's growing sense, which was to become chronic in the post-war era, of being completely over-whelmed by current events, and which led him to concentrate, in his unfinished novel, on episodes set in the age before 1914.

Despite its imperfections, *Les Thibault* can sustain comparison with any modern novel of similar scope and form. It needs to be compared not with *A la Recherche du Temps Perdu*, which studies a different subject and represents an almost totally different aesthetic, but with those cyclical novels which portray, for the most part, middle-class characters in a solidly physical world. Of these bourgeois family-chroniclers, Martin du Gard is probably to-day the least read yet the most readable: he could create character and compose dramatic scenes as successfully as any of his contemporaries; with *L'Eté 1914*, he added a dimension and a power to *Les Thibault* which are denied to Thomas Mann's *Buddenbrooks* or Galsworthy's *Forsyte Saga*; the two excellent volumes devoted to the Battle of Verdun in *Les Hommes de Bonne Volonté* vie with *L'Eté 1914* in sweep and force, but Romains' vast novel-cycle lacks the unity and compactness of Martin du Gard's; the humanistic pessimism of *Les Thibault*, which has worn rather better than the ardent idealism of *Jean Christophe* or the cosy sentimentality of *La Chronique des Pasquier*, has much in common with the outlook of Camus and Malraux: Jacques Thibault is probably the most important literary progenitor of Meursault, and *L'Eté 1914* is at least the equal of *La Condition Humaine*. What Martin du Gard said of *L'Eté 1914* during his Nobel Prize speech in 1937 has no less tragic relevance to-day:

"In this exceptionally grave period humanity is passing through, I wish—I say this without vanity, but from the very depths of a heart that is heavy with anxiety—I wish for my books on the summer of 1914 to be read and discussed, and for them to remind everyone, both the old who have forgotten and the young who never knew, of the moving lesson of the past."*

* *Loc. cit.*, p. 360.

is the only reliable guide, the one unimpeachable witness, for it is there that even the most secretive of artists removes his mask and, in spite of himself, reveals his secret."*

Though Martin du Gard warned critics not to be over-hasty in identifying him with any of his characters, it seems safe to assume that if, from work to work they continue to pursue the same ideals, they are likely to express certain of the essential preoccupations of their creator. It is of considerable significance, therefore, that each of the protagonists in *Devenir! Jean Barois*, and *Les Thibault* should reject any supernatural account of the Universe and seek purely human solutions to the major problems that confront them: it is no less significant that all their efforts should end in humiliating failure. Each of them stresses, or is warned, that self-knowledge is the key to all forms of human achievement: "The difficult thing is to be true to oneself, resolutely enough and long enough to discover how to be really authentic," Bernard Grosdidier says to the hero of *Devenir!*, and he adds with characteristic pessimism, "Nearly everyone fails" (*O.C.*, I, p. 24). Luce, Jean Barois, and Jacques Thibault state this same basic axiom in almost the same terms and with the same gloomy rejoinder. The most important message Antoine Thibault believes he can leave for his nephew, Jean-Paul, is

* Quoted in *La Nouvelle Revue Française*, December 1958, p. 965.

the importance of self-knowledge and the difficulty of acquiring it: he dies confessing that he has never really been able to understand himself or the world about him. Armand, one of the minor characters in *Un Taciturne*, whose sardonic humour has much in common with Martin du Gard's own, reflects: "Your life is played out before your eyes like a charade . . . You spend your time looking for the answer to the riddle . . . Some people even find it, right at the end, when it's too late to be of any use" (*O.C.*, II, p. 1196).

Martin du Gard's central characters have even less success in understanding other people than in understanding themselves, and for this reason they are doomed to unhappiness in love. In Martin du Gard's world lasting satisfaction in love seems impossible chiefly because the basic aims of his men and women are utterly opposed. All his heroines are ready to consider the world well lost for love: Ketty Varine (*Devenir!*), Julia (*Jean Barois*), the prostitute who seduces the schoolboy Daniel (*Le Cahier gris*), Lisbeth (*Le Pénitencier*), Rachel and Rinette (*La Belle Saison*), Anne de Battaincourt (*La Consultation*, *L'Eté 1914*), Amalia (*Confidence Africaine*), Isabelle and Wanda (*Un Taciturne*)—all these are powerfully sensual women, each ready to take the initiative, each prepared to sacrifice all moral scruples and conventional self-restraint to gratify their physical appetites once these have been aroused. Thérèse and Jenny de Fontanin have the same passionate natures and are able to dominate them only by the inhibiting power of their no less passionate puritanism. But while love, to Martin du Gard's women characters, is or could easily become their whole existence, to Barois and the Thibault brothers it can never be more than a brief diversion from their life's work. The only occasion when they are as passionately stirred as their partners is when they find themselves together in the presence of death or mortal danger: Barois first embraces Cécile as they stand at the bedside of his dying father, and he and Julia first feel intense physical desire for each other as a violent mob threatens to wreck the *Semeur* office; Jacques is seduced by Lisbeth immediately after the death of her aunt, and finally consummates his love with Jenny soon after the death of her father, when Europe is clearly intent on plunging into war; Antoine's passionate love-affair with Rachel begins immediately after, even in the course of, his dramatic fight to save a child's life, and he first feels violently attracted to Anne de Battaincourt when she pays her respects after the death of his father. For Martin du Gard's heroes, however, these are quite exceptional occasions: sexual indulgence is necessary to them, but it is never allowed to distract them for long from their main quest for integrity and truth.

For this same reason, Martin du Gard's protagonists all show a marked reluctance to take on marital responsibility: in *Devenir!* Mazerelles deserts Ketty Varine because she is so manifestly intent on marrying him, and he is finally persuaded to marry Denise Herzeaux only because of the lure of her attractive dowry; in *Jean Barois* Barois abruptly ends a youthful liaison with Huguette because he feels too domesticated; the section of the novel dealing with his marriage is significantly entitled *The Chain*, has for epigraph a sentence from Herzog, "Marriage is a danger only to the man who has ideas", and contains extracts from Jean's diary, in which he scorns women for what he considers to be their incurable sentimentality and their irremediable intellectual inferiority. None of the major characters in *Les Thibault* finds a happy or lasting love. Monsieur Thibault has known married happiness, but has already been a widower for fourteen years when the action of the novel begins; the marriages of the Fontanin parents, of Pastor Gregory, of Rachel, and of Anne de Battaincourt are all utter failures; Jacques, Antoine, Gise, and Daniel never marry, while Jenny reveals such marked aversion for physical contact that any sort of normal marriage for her seems quite inconceivable.

If, for the most part, Martin du Gard's men and women are predestined to failure in love because of mutual incompatibility, there remains an important minority group whose unhappiness is guaranteed because they have far too much in common. In *Les Thibault*, for example, though normal adolescent or mature heterosexual relationships predominate, there is a remarkable recurrence of the theme of incest: Hirsch, Rachel's daemonic lover, drives his own daughter to suicide after making love to her on her honeymoon; Antoine is at one point very strongly attracted to Gise, whom both the brothers always look upon as their sister; Gise falls hopelessly in love with Jacques, whom she treats as a brother; *La Sorellina*, the short story partly inspired by Jacques' feelings for Gise, describes a violent incestuous passion that is eventually consummated, and Jacques comes to believe that Jenny's temperament is so similar to his own that it is rather more than a conventional lover's expression when he declares that they are twin souls.

Martin du Gard returned to the theme of incest in 1930 with *Confidence Africaine*, a short, remarkably matter-of-fact account, told in the first person by an Italian, Leandro Barbazano, of a lyrical love-affair with his own sister Amalia, which began when they were a pair of hot-blooded adolescents forced to share the same small bedroom in their father's over-crowded North African flat.

In 1931, while convalescing after the serious car-crash that led him to replan *Les Thibault*, he wrote *Un Taciturne*. This is a three-act play which portrays a network of human relationships more intricate and, because of the limitations imposed by the medium of the drama, more tightly knit than that in *Les Thibault*. Thierry, an enigmatic business man who has never married, engages a young man, Joe, as his private secretary. Joe falls in love with Thierry's sister, Isabelle, who at first repulses him because of the guilt she feels about her murky past: she has been imprisoned in a reform-school because when she was a schoolgirl she tried to murder one of her friends in a fit of Lesbian jealousy; this friend, scarred for life, has remained an intimate member of the family circle and is still in love with her. When, finally, Joe is able to announce to Thierry that he has discovered Isabelle's secret, overcome her scruples, and persuaded her to marry him, Thierry suddenly realizes that he has been in love with Joe all along, and either because of shame or jealous despair, he shoots himself.

The play was not a conspicuous success when it was produced by Jouvet at the Comédie des Champs-Elysées in October 1931, with himself in the tailor-made rôle of Armand, Thierry's middle-aged business partner, who hides his hopeless love for Isabelle beneath a façade of sardonic humour. The fault was probably neither in the construction, which is much more competent than a bald synopsis can indicate, nor in the characterization, though Thierry's prolonged self-deception and Joe's powers of attraction seem more than a little implausible. What most limited the appeal of the play was probably its anachronistic *ethos*: with its plethora of minute stage-directions, its unrelieved gloom, its stress on the inevitable consequences of heredity, it was really designed to be staged not at the Comédie des Champs Elysées in 1931, but by the *Théâtre Libre* in the 1890s where Martin du Gard, as a faithful patron, served his dramatist's apprenticeship.

Martin du Gard does not view sexual relationships, whether normal or abnormal, legal or illicit, with any of the mingled relish and distaste that characterizes the treatment of such subjects in the works of Zola, Gide, or Mauriac. Sexual passion may, in certain parts of Martin du Gard's work, stimulate over-lurid flights of imagination, but it is never a subject for prurient gloating or righteous indignation. In his frank *Notes sur André Gide*, he takes a very much more serious view of his friend's continual self-dramatization than of his sexual misadventures: these are censured only because of the probable suffering they inflicted on Madame Gide, not because they are held to be wrong in themselves. "These things seem to happen quite naturally," says Leandro, discussing his incestuous love-affair with his own sister. "It's all perfectly simple really, when you think about it, if you see how one thing leads to another" (*O.C.*, II, p. 1121). Armand makes almost the same resigned comment on Thierry's homosexuality as he does on middle-aged men who take to collecting obscene photographs: "These things just happen, you know—they can happen to perfectly respectable people . . ." (O.C., II, p. 1346). Like Leandro and Armand, and like Antoine uncovering his patients' sordid secrets in *La Consultation*, Martin du Gard seems to have viewed deviations from the norm with compassion and with complete amorality, accepting them, like the sexual norm itself, as an inescapable part of human experience.

In his treatment of religious or political problems Martin du Gard preserves almost the same equanimity: he makes every conceivable effort to give a full, fair hearing to each side in any dispute, neither priests nor free-thinkers, neither bourgeois nor Marxists are allowed a monopoly of either virtues or vices. Though his Left Wing, humanistic sympathies are occasionally too strong to be disguised in *Jean Barois* and *Les Thibault*, in both these works he fully justifies his own description of himself as "a writer without prejudice . . . an independent who has freed himself from the fascination of any partisan ideology", one of those "whose constant care is to develop their personal conscience, in order to keep their inquiring mind as objective, as emancipated, and as fair as is humanly possible".*

On one topic, however, Martin du Gard seems to have been quite unable to remain impartial. One section of the community remained in his

* Nobel Prize Speech, *loc. cit.*, p. 958.

view the subject for either coarse humour—the only humour in his work, in fact, apart from the inconsiderable eccentricities of Monsieur Chasles —or savage satire: these were the French peasants.

Martin du Gard's two rural farces, both written as a diversion from the prosperous bourgeois world in which he spent his life and which he chose to portray in each of his major novels, were both composed in authentic Berrichon dialect. Both recall medieval *fabliaux*, with the unequivocal earthiness of their language and situations and the guilt and rapacity of their peasant protagonists. In *Le Testament du Père Leleu*, Alexandre, an old countryman, dies without leaving a will; Torine, who for long has acted as his servant and his concubine, on the tacit understanding that she is to be his sole legatee, decides not to report his death until old Leleu, a neighbour who bears a striking resemblance to Alexandre, has impersonated the dead man in the village notary's presence and drawn up a will in her favour. Leleu agrees to the masquerade, but outwits his accomplice by willing both the chattels and Torine to his real self. *La Gonfle* is rather more indelicate in language and situation, and has never been acted: La Bique,* a possessive spinster, is suffer-

* It is not easy to find a concise English way of conveying the ripe vulgarity of this name: the feminine definite article employed before a surname expresses disrespect. "Bique" is "a nanny goat": "Old Ma Nanny Goat" might, therefore, be the nearest equivalent.

ing from acute dropsy; her servant girl, La Nioule, a deaf mute, is pregnant either by the local veterinary surgeon, Gustave, who is La Bique's nephew, or by Andoche, her handyman and paramour, who is also the village sacristan. The action is completely dominated by Andoche, who extracts the maximum personal benefit from the situation, and recounts a great number of scabrous stories while his various plots are being hatched: Gustave is persuaded, by fear of scandal and hope of reward, to administer an anaesthetic to both women, to relieve La Bique of her dropsy and to deliver La Nioule of her baby, which is at once transported to the bed of her still unconscious employer: Andoche thus averts the danger of losing his job for having seduced La Nioule and, by claiming to be the father of La Bique's child, ensures that she will marry him and so give him complete charge of her possessions.

In *Vieille France*, which Martin du Gard wrote at Sauveterre in the spring of 1932 after destroying *L'Appareillage*, the humour is no less earthy but very much more sardonic. Like *La Consultation* or *Le Diable Boiteux*, it describes the hidden and, for the most part, sordid lives of the outwardly respectable citizens with whom the central character comes into contact in the course of a single day. Martin du Gard's Astaroth is Joigneau, postman to the imaginary village of Maupeyrou, and by the time his daily round is over, the secrets of every household have been laid bare. There is not a single contented character in the whole community, and scarcely a virtuous one: the younger wives and husbands all lust after their neighbours' bodies and worldly goods, and are all unfaithful and dishonest in thought if not in deed; the young people think only of escaping to the bright lights of the city, the old live in squalor and look to death for merciful release. Everyone is consumed with either envy or lust or malice or physical decay: the postman who dominates the action is different from the others only because he is more cunning, more grasping, and more actively lecherous than the rest. There are only two small centres of comparative enlightenment in this primeval jungle, and they themselves are menaced from within by disillusionment: these are the village church, attended only by prurient old maids and by sex-starved war-widows, where the village curé has long since turned his back on his flock to devote all his attention to his gardening, and the village school, where the frustrated schoolmaster and his sister are saved from total despair only by their Marxist hopes that their fellowmen will be miraculously transformed by social revolution.

In *Vieille France* Martin du Gard has clearly abandoned the principles of impersonality and benign equanimity which play so conspicuous a part in shaping all his other work. His overt satirical intentions are conveyed not only by the relish with which he highlights every ugly defect, or by the care he takes to suppress every possible redeeming virtue of country life, but by a variety of minute details. By what are obviously his own personal interpolations: thus, the clerical Church clock is always *"naturally"* ten minutes slower than the clock on the Republican schoolhouse; the inside window-sills of the *bien-pensant* Madame Massot are strewn with dead flies, "they died," observes the narrator, "of sheer boredom"; Joseph, the young apprentice who lodges with Joigneau, pauses for a moment outside the bedroom door behind which waits Madame Joigneau, only too eager to pay back her husband for his many acts of infidelity; Joseph, however, innocently decides to continue his way upstairs, followed by what can only be the author's comment, "The fool!" Other ways in which Martin du Gard expresses his irony are the figures of speech he occasionally employs, zeugma particularly: thus, "Madame Massot knits away, shut away inside her room and her deafness"; and Tulle, a one-armed war-veteran, is said to be supported by "France and his sister, Madame Bosse". But what most eloquently conveys Martin du Gard's distaste for the characters he is portraying is his use of animal-imagery.

Animal-imagery is sometimes applied to characters in *Les Thibault*: thus the eyes of

Mademoiselle de Waize, the Thibault family housekeeper, are said to be like a doe's when she is in repose, but like a hen's when she is startled; Gise's eyes are compared to those of a faithful dog; Alfreda, Meynestrel's faithless mistress, is likened to a cat; a nameless waitress in a restaurant where Jacques and Jenny dine on the eve of war is compared to a grazing heifer; l'abbé Binet, the most unpleasant of Jacques' schoolteachers, is likened to a mongrel cur; Monsieur Chasles, to a slinking rat; and Pastor Gregory, to both a spider and a monkey. It is noticeable, however, that these are all minor characters, and that the undistinguished animal similes are employed in the main for mildly comic purposes. In *Vieille France* Martin du Gard's use of animal-imagery to describe the physical or moral deficiencies of his villagers is at once more savage and more systematic. Scarcely a single inhabitant of Maupeyrou is spared: Joigneau, the arch-schemer, is likened to a spider spinning a web; Loutre, the market-gardener, has a neck like a chicken; Mademoiselle Ennberg, the schoolmistress, has the jaws of a pike; Bosse, the café-owner, has eyes like a frog, his wife resembles a black hen forever about to peck; in a sustained simile half a page long Madame Xavier, who keeps the local grocery, is likened to a cat; Madame Daigne, who has independent means, has bald patches on her skull, "as pink as a piglet's skin"; the curé is always sniffing and shaking himself like a dog just out of water; Mademoiselle Massot, a bigoted spinster nick-named "Espérance", has withers like a horse; Madame Flamart, who keeps a roadside café, has nostrils like a heifer, while her frequently cuckolded husband has every bull-like attribute except potency; Madame Touche, one of three embittered war-widows, has cheeks like cutlets of raw veal; Monsieur des Navières, who in his senile decay keeps a tormented vigil over the worthless pieces of rubbish he imagines to be valuable antiques, "swallows back his saliva with the noise a carp makes as it sucks a piece of moist bread". The whole work, Martin du Gard declared in the brief description he com-posed for advance publicity purposes, was meant to portray "a swarm of microbes in a drop of stagnant water".

Because of its sustained virulence, *Vieille France* occupies a unique place among Martin du Gard's works. It makes the same scathing indictment of French country life as *Les Paysans* of Balzac, as *La Terre*, as the rural *contes* of Mau-passant, but it is not a mere pastiche: it is the deliberate expression of bitter personal anti-pathy. In a letter to Jean Schlumberger he described *Vieille France* as "a picture gallery filled with ugly faces and cold, cruel, greedy hearts—a world impossible to defend".* When

* Quoted in *La Nouvelle Revue Française*, December 1958, p. 1063.

he was criticized by Marcel Arland for drawing such a gloomy picture of French country life Martin du Gard felt obliged, for the only time in his long career, to explain his motives in a letter to the Press. "Even though one examines that accursed race [of peasants] with all one's love for one's fellow-men," he wrote in *La Nouvelle Revue Française* in June 1933, "it is rare indeed to find the slightest spark of decency. . . ." "I did not think people would find any cruelty in my book," he said in this same letter, "I thought they would be struck only by its note of despair."*

One probable cause for this despair is likely to have been Martin du Gard's bitter realization of the profound gulf between his adult and his childhood vision of the world. To the dis-illusioned middle-aged author of *Vieille France* the villagers were squirrels in a cage, the countrywomen as industrious and inhuman as ants, and all of them were inhabitants of a world where "everybody thinks only of himself, of his own paltry little business, his own paltry little savings, his own paltry little security".† But in

---

* To judge from the reviews of the English translation of *Vieille France*, first published in 1954 with the title of *The Postman*, English critics seem on the whole to have detected no despair in the work whatsoever. An anony-mous reviewer in *The Times* found Maupeyrou "a bright little, tight little world", and that Martin du Gard had described it "with an almost innocent and disarming gaiety"!

† *La Nouvelle Française*, June 1933.

Noizemont-les-Vierges,* a little-known fragment of thinly disguised autobiography not included in the Pléiade edition of his *Œuvres Complètes*, Martin du Gard wrote in completely different spirit of his maternal great grandmother's house in Clermont (Oise) where, as a child, he regularly used to spend his summer holidays:

"I think of the kind words, the traditional jokes, and the mutual understanding which truly united those simple, sincere and upright folk, whose faults remained socially acceptable and did not degenerate into vices; I think of the dignity, the reserve, the fundamental nobility of that healthy little world, where money and business matters were kept in their place and which were never allowed to corrupt; I think of those lives, often arduous but never wavering from the path of righteousness, and which were never attacked by parasitical ambition, which were dedicated to each day's humble task if not without effort, then at least without baseness or resentment. They spent their time giving pleasure to others, love to their children, encouragement to the workers,

* Martin du Gard wrote this chapter of autobiography in the Rhineland while awaiting demobilization at the beginning of 1919. In 1926 he found himself threatened with a court-action by a young Belgian publisher for failing to supply him, as he had contracted to do, with a short text for his series of limited editions. The only solution Martin du Gard could devise was to change a few unimportant details in his autobiographical fragment, and the result was published in Liège in 1928.

help to the needy. For sixty years without a break, they had remained loyal to the same principles of fair play, and to the same laws of domestic honour, and they looked on the approach of old age as the coming of autumn after the season of flowers. I think how authentic it all was, and I pay tribute to that incomparable wealth of goodness, that perfect example of social harmony, which lasted for a brief while only and now seems past beyond recall. . . ." (*Noizemont-les-Vierges*, pp. 38–9).

The ferocity of *Vieille France* is without parallel elsewhere in Martin du Gard's work, except for the closing chapters of *L'Eté 1914*, where it is probably no mere coincidence that Jacques' tormentors and his cowardly executioner are French peasants. It can be partly explained as anger over the betrayal of a childhood ideal. It also expresses the bitterness of a disillusioned humanist who has been confronted with the living disproof of his belief that Man is something higher than the beasts of the field.

In the letter he wrote in 1933 to defend *Vieille France*, Martin du Gard insisted that he had not intended to satirize the whole of humanity, merely the French peasant; he maintained that he had high hopes of the urban proletariat and that if genuine Socialism were allowed to transform the world, mankind would reveal undreamed-of unselfish, fraternal, and possibly even spiritual qualities. This view is expressed recurrently throughout Martin du Gard's novels, but with significantly less confidence in his later work: in *Jean Barois* Marc-Elie Luce and the *Semeur* group are serene in their conviction that world social revolution will inevitably bring about a moral rejuvenation of the human race; Mademoiselle Ennberg, the Marxist schoolmistress in *Vieille France*, is much less optimistic:

"She broods over her loneliness, over the life of the village, over this bestial humanity still crawling in the lower depths. Why is the world like this? Is it really the fault of society? . . . And the terrifying question she has so often asked herself returns to haunt her once more: 'Is the fault not really in mankind itself?' But she has in her heart such a need for faith and so much innocent fervour, that she cannot bring herself to doubt in human nature. No, no! . . . Only let a new social order come into being— better organized, less irrational, less unjust—and perhaps at last Man will show what he is really capable of" (*O.C.*, II, p. 1102).

Jacques Thibault clings no less desperately to his Socialist hopes because they are all that give his life any purpose, but only intermittently can he feel any confidence in Mankind itself: "He felt infinite pity for his fellow-men, but he remained sceptical about their moral possibilities" (*O.C.*, II, p. 164); and his scepticism is amply justified when the nations of Europe march so eagerly to war, and when, as he lies dying after

107

his futile leaflet flight, hostile peasants refuse to give him a drink, and burn him with lighted cigarette stubs. The war destroys Antoine's faith in the unbounded powers of Science as it destroys Jacques' faith in the strength of international Socialism. Antoine dies, willing himself to believe in Humanity, but like Voltaire at the end of his *Essai sur les Mœurs*, appalled by the spectacle of the docility of the common people in the clutches of their rulers, and all too grimly aware of the thousands of years that must still elapse before Reason can bring about the reign of universal brotherhood on earth.

The greatest single cause of both individual and international suffering in Martin du Gard's world is not the wilful malice of his characters, but their helplessness against the blind and omnipotent forces of determinism: Barois is foredoomed to failure because the lessons of his Catholic upbringing leave as permanent an imprint on his mind as his grave childhood illness on his body; Jacques Thibault is driven to become a Socialist rebel because of his father's tyranny and the insensitivity of his Catholic schoolteachers; Antoine is shocked to discover, as he lies dying, that he has unconsciously adopted the laugh and speech-habits of his father; the Fontanin children inherit their parents' passionate natures, but because of their mother's different attitude to them both, Daniel becomes a lecher and Jenny grows up a prude; Thierry and his father both commit suicide because they fall hopelessly in love with their secretary; Michel Luzzato is condemned to a sickly life and an early death because his parents were brother and sister. The nations are no less subject to the rigorous rule of determinism than individuals: Jacques and Antoine both conclude that the First World War was mainly caused neither by the machinations of a few evil statesmen, nor by over-pugnacious General Staffs, nor even by the effects of international capitalism, but by the inability of the human race to evolve beyond its tribal past. Propagandists of each State can always make a successful appeal to the primitive pride and fears of their citizens, because in all men lurks a powerful atavistic urge to destroy: Philip, the most outstanding clinician in *Les Thibault*, reflects: "Perhaps the instinctive urge to destroy, the periodic need to bring crashing to the ground all that we have so laboriously raised up, is one of the fundamental laws which impose a limit on the constructive possibilities of our nature. Perhaps this is one of those mysterious and galling laws which the wise man must recognize and accept" (*O.C.*, II, p. 900). Philip is as much admired by Antoine as Marc-Elie Luce by Barois, and it is difficult to avoid the conclusion that, with Luce, he is the character who most directly expresses the views of Martin du Gard himself.

It was not, however, his belief in universal determinism that most dominated Martin du

Gard's thought and work. He noted in 1918: "I realize that *all my life*, the whole secret of my life (and also of my artistic vocation, of my will to survive), the motive force of all my efforts, the source of all my emotions is my *fear of death*, my struggle against oblivion, dust and Time."* His lifelong preoccupation with death is apparent from the remarkable amount of space it occupies in his work: in *Noizemont-les-Vierges* he reveals that as a very young child one of the favourite haunts during his school holidays was the village cemetery, and that his first awareness of the reality of death came just after the funeral service for his beloved grandmother; in his discarded youthful novel, *Marise*, he planned to study the old age and death of his heroine with particular care; Denise Mazerelles in *Devenir!*, Luce, Jean Barois and his father, M. Thibault, Jacques, Antoine, Jérôme de Fontanin, his mistress Noémie, Nicole's baby daughter—the deaths of each of these are not only described in minute detail but inspire his most powerful writing.

What most fascinated Martin du Gard was not so much the physical processes of death, as the emotional responses of the dying person. Like Montaigne, he considered that "he who could teach men how to die, would teach them how to live". His main characters all search for a faith that will enable them to die with peace and

* Quoted in *La Nouvelle Revue Française*, December 1958, pp. 971–2.

dignity, and it is clearly indicative of Martin du Gard's own personal views that while his Catholics, Barois and Monsieur Thibault, die hysterically, his rationalists, Luce and Antoine, die with unruffled calm. Their quiet acceptance of death was the ideal that Martin du Gard himself aspired to in life: he was particularly inspired by his former—Catholic—schoolteacher, l'abbé Hébert, whose serenely Socratic approach to death provided the model for the death of Marc-Elie Luce, and by the last moments of Gide, whose death he witnessed. "To see such a calm death, does one good," he declared at the end of his *Notes sur André Gide*. "This renunciation and this exemplary acceptance of the natural law are contagious. We must be infinitely grateful to him for having been able to die so *well*" (*O.C.*, II, p. 1423). All the evidence that has been made available since his own death suggests that Martin du Gard approached it with the same serenity as the most stoical of his characters and his friends.

Because, throughout his career, Martin du Gard remained convinced of the omnipotence of determinism and the finality of death, and could find no consolation in any scientific, political, or religious beliefs, it is scarcely surprising that the most distinctive quality of his thought and of his work should be pessimism. The ambitions of all his characters are for the most part cruelly thwarted: Mazerelles never becomes a great writer; the materialist testament of Barois and the pacifist tracts of Jacques Thibault, the writings they most want to be read, are destroyed before they reach their public; Antoine is struck down in the prime of life with his dreams of fame unrealized, and like Jérôme de Fontanin and Thierry, he takes his own life. Martin du Gard's personal despair is given distinctive stress, however, not only by the number of agonizing deaths and suicides in his works but by the scenes and images which so often end them: the closing words of *L'Été 1914*, "*Fumier! Fumier! Fumier!*" which serve as ordinary mankind's final comment on Jacques' foolhardy bid to avert war; Armand's bitter cry of "*L'imbècile!*" on which the final curtain descends on *Un Taciturne*, after Thierry has just committed suicide; Mademoiselle Ennberg's nightmare at the end of *Vieille France* when she, the most fervent guardian of what little human decency there is in the village, dreams her brother is strangling his wife with a clothes-line. Each of these is as telling as the last line of a successful sonnet or the final fade-out shot of a well-made film.

Certain of Martin du Gard's other works, however, end on a slightly less despairing note: the servant girl watching Mazerelles from the window, at the end of *Devenir!* and who, it is subtly implied, will sooner or later console him for the loss of his wife; the scene that concludes *Confidence Africaine*, in which the hero's sister, transformed from a lithe adolescent to an obese matron, is seen suckling a gluttonous infant; Antoine's last message to Jean-Paul, telling him that he must pass on the torch of life to his son in turn, even though its purpose might for ever elude him. These conclusions express the last meagre hope that the humanist still desperately clings to, when confronted with such abundant evidence of man's inhumanity and of God's indifference to man: the irrational faith that though human lives may be destroyed, Life itself goes on, probably imperfectible and, in the pre-nuclear age when Martin du Gard was writing, seemingly indestructible.

Conclusion

That Martin du Gard had certain outstanding literary qualities can scarcely be denied. His narrative gifts are admirably displayed in *La Belle Saison*, *La Mort du Père*, and *Confidence Africaine*; his well-developed powers of observation are clearly revealed in the remarkably perspicacious *Notes sur André Gide* or in the minutely composed portraits of the members of the Thibault family; his sensibility and compassion are revealed in his many analyses of complex human relationships and, in particular, in his studies of adolescence; his genuine dramatic sense is exhibited not only in each of his plays but also in the scenic construction of *Jean Barois*, *Les Thibault*, and *Vieille France*; his ability to impose order and pattern on a vast mass of inchoate documents is shown in the structure of *Jean Barois* and *L'Eté 1914*. He collected his background material more diligently and utilized it more intelligently than the Goncourts or Zola. Seldom distracted by illness or material difficulties, he was able to devote almost the whole of his long life to literature. Why, then, should his work have made so limited an impact on the public of yesterday and to-day?

A partial explanation can be found in Martin du Gard's adherence to outmoded or unrewarding literary theories: his insistence on reconstructing the crumbling bourgeois world of the 1890–1914 period, when the sophisticated public had come to expect the serious novelist to explore the twilight regions of the mind, like Proust or Joyce, or to express contemporary *angoisse*, like Kafka or Sartre or Camus; his devotion to the cult of impersonality which resulted in a prose style so chastened, so purged of images and idio-syncrasies as to seem devoid of all character; his deliberate policy of mirroring banal reality without transfiguring it, so that Barois and Antoine Thibault, who largely dominate his two major works are, because of the thorough-ness with which he put his theories into effect, quite unexceptional and quite unmemor-able.

But Martin du Gard's literary principles and practice were alike determined by what is still the most enigmatic thing about him, his own elusive personality, and this it is that must be held re-sponsible for the main limitations of his work. He would seem to have been one of the most thorough-going pessimists in the history of the French novel. Unlike Flaubert or Proust, who in all other respects were as nihilistic as he, he had no great faith in the literature to which he de-voted the whole of his long career: the technical problems of novel-writing simply proved to be a useful substitute for religious or political belief, but he was too profoundly sceptical ever to elevate them to the level of a mystique.

Martin du Gard's ever-present scepticism brought both rewards and penalties: it prevented him from committing the naïve intellectual errors of so many of his nineteenth-century predecessors, but at the same time, it deprived his work of that infectious enthusiasm which, in the novels of Balzac or Dickens or Tolstoy or Zola, the majority of readers find a more than adequate compensation. There is no poetry, no gusto and scarcely any humour in Martin du Gard's major works, and as realistic studies of the whole range of human experience, therefore, they cannot fail to seem deficient when set beside *War and Peace* or *A la Recherche du Temps Perdu*.

It was this same all-corrosive scepticism, turned to bear on his own grandiose ambitions, which so seriously curtailed Martin du Gard's literary production, and caused him to revise and reject so many carefully nurtured plans. His uncertainty about the true nature of his vocation, seen in the three false starts he made at the beginning of his career, in his renunciation of the documentary novel in 1918, his return to it in *L'Eté 1914*, and his renewed dissatisfaction with it in the late 1930s, was even more pronounced in his literary activities after *Les Thibault* was completed. In February 1940 he wrote to Gide announcing that he had, after much thought, finally given up his long-cherished plan of writing a large-scale novel about old age. He noted in his Journal in May 1941 that he had begun several other books and scrapped them all. In the summer of 1946 he noted that he had made a number of attempts to write a play about the youth of the post-war world, and finally abandoned the project. But his most spectacular failure was undoubtedly his inability to conclude, possibly even to begin, the vast novel to which he devoted almost all his attention from the winter of 1941 till shortly before his death in August 1958.

The difficulties Martin du Gard encountered in planning and writing this novel are described in the extracts from his journal and from his correspondence with Gide, which together make up the last third of the *Souvenirs Littéraires*. For many years this novel bore the title *Le Journal du Colonel Maumort*: the hero was to have been a retired Army colonel who, when the Germans over-ran France in the summer of 1940, destroys the private journal he has kept assiduously since his youth. He quickly regrets his over-hasty action, and tries to reconstruct his journal by the protracted exercise of memory. Martin du Gard's commentary on his aims and problems in describing Maumort's life's work show that he was as perplexed at the end of his career about his own true gifts and his best course of action as he had been, intermittently, ever since he first decided to write: he insists repeatedly on the necessity for meticulous planning, on the vital necessity of copious historical documentation, on the attention he must pay to chronology; to guarantee complete objectivity he composes a minutely detailed account of Maumort's life, from his birth till his seventieth year, even though large tracts of it will never be utilized for the final novel. What, however, most impeded Martin du Gard's progress was not the inordinate stress he laid on his preparatory work but his inability to impose definitive form upon it: Maumort's life story was originally to have been described in a journal, then in a series of *nouvelles* written in the third person, and later by means of letters exchanged between Maumort and an intimate friend: by 1955, as the final entry in the *Souvenirs* reveals, this plan too was eventually given up in despair.

It is clear from a number of references in the *Souvenirs* that Martin du Gard's chronic indecision was not caused by purely technical factors. Setting himself intricate literary problems provided a most convenient distraction from the thought of old age and his inevitable death. He noted with characteristic lucidity as early as July 1942: "This vast project is like a screen between myself and the future, between myself and decrepitude, between myself and approaching death. That terrifying thought of Pascal's comes to mind: 'We rush on heedlessly towards the abyss, after placing something before our eyes to prevent our seeing it'" (*O.C.*, I, p. cviii). With each succeeding year, he grew less and less interested in the world around him, more and more determined that *Maumort* should not be published till long after his death. He noted in his journal in 1948: "How incomparably soothing it is to write a work that will only be published posthumously" (*O.C.*, I, p. cxxxvii). The last few months of his life were spent calmly collecting and classifying his papers, before sealing them away in the Bibliothèque Nationale for at least twenty-five years.

Martin du Gard's own view of *Maumort* was characteristically pessimistic: he remained convinced that it could only have interested readers of 1910, and that its value was bound to be strictly limited. "I know well enough that if I have time to finish it," he noted in his journal in 1947, "my book will have some qualities. But even if such a book comes off, it may well not shed the slightest glimmer of fresh light on human truth. In that case, why should I bother to write it? What point would there be in repeating what has been already said? What a comfort it would be if one could be deluded into believing that one was going to add just a tiny new shade of colour to the solar spectrum" (*O.C.*, I, p. cxxxii). Whether this gloomy appraisal was justified cannot be decided till the *Maumort* manuscripts are published.*   In the meantime, scholars and critics must wait like the pupils of old Frehnhofer in Balzac's story *Le Chef d'Œuvre Inconnu*: their master worked in secret for ten years on a picture he claimed would be his supreme masterpiece; when at last his canvas was revealed it proved to be a chaotic mass of lines, yet in one corner of the picture was a foot, so superbly executed that the viewers could only marvel at its perfection.

Although Gide preferred what he was shown of *Maumort* to any of Martin du Gard's other writings, Martin du Gard's own descriptions of his preparatory work for it suggest that it is similar in character to *Jean Barois* and *Les Thibault*, drawing heavily on historical documentation and bearing only a faint imprint of the author's own personality.   In his *Souvenirs* Martin du Gard quotes from a letter he received in 1920 from his son-in-law, Marcel de Coppet, praising the technical competence of *Le Cahier Gris* but deploring the effects of his over-zealous adherence to the cult of impersonality:

"As soon as you start to write as a novelist, it is just as though the strain of composing, your technical ingenuity and your excessive concern for polishing and for never losing control, all stifle certain of your original gifts and makes your writing commonplace. . . . This lack of

* An edition in two volumes is being prepared by Pierre Herbart.

genuine originality and spark grieves me, because I know it is not due to any deficiency in your own personality, but the result of a sort of refusal on your part to give free rein to your natural flowing style" (*O.C.*, I, p. lxxxv).

Reflecting on this observation in 1955, Martin du Gard commented: "This criticism troubled me profoundly at the time and, if the truth be told, it has never since ceased to worry me" (*ibid.*). How accurate a diagnosis it was will be finally established only with the publication of Martin du Gard's journal, now sealed away in the Bibliothèque Nationale for twenty-five years, and of the many letters in the possession of his friends or their executors. The extracts so far published of his journal, in particular, his composite portraits of Gide, Copeau, and Paul Desjardins, show him to have been an extremely shrewd observer of his contemporaries; the very few of his many letters that have so far been made available give some indication of the warm personality and vigorous stylist that were deliberately effaced whenever he wrote a novel or play.

It is perhaps a portent that Martin du Gard's own account of his long, vain struggle to crown his career with a final great masterpiece should be, beyond dispute, so much more poignant than the journal he composed for the dying Antoine. One may be justified in speculating, therefore, whether Martin du Gard, who shared Flaubert's love of seclusion, his preoccupation with technique, his profound pessimism, and his cult of impersonality, will, like Flaubert, ultimately win much wider posthumous fame when his hidden self is revealed through his correspondence.

Biographical Notes

1881   Born 23rd March at 69 boulevard Bineau, Neuilly-sur-Seine, into a family connected for generations with the legal profession.

1892–8   Studies at l'école Fénelon, lycée Condorcet, and lycée Janson-de-Sailly.

1903–5   At Ecole des Chartes; qualifies as archivist and palaeographer with a thesis on the ruins of the Norman abbey at Jumièges.

1906   Marries Hélène Foucault, daughter of a Paris barrister; plans and starts work on *Une Vie de Saint*.

1907   Birth of daughter, Christiane.

1908   Abandons *Une Vie de Saint*; writes *Devenir!* in a few weeks.

1909   Begins and soon abandons new novel, *Marise*.

1910–13   At work on *Jean Barois* at le Verger d'Augy, Sancergues, in Cher département.

1913   Writes *Le Testament du Père Leleu* in August; first meets Gide, November.

1914–18   Serves throughout war as sergeant with a motor-transport unit.

1919	Demobilized; begins to write journal, which he keeps till 1949.
1920	Draws up complete plan for *Les Thibault*; moves to Clermont in Oise département.
1922	First of many visits to *décades de Pontigny*; writes first version of *La Gonfle*.
1924	Father dies of stroke, aged 68.
1925	Mother dies of cancer, aged 65; R.M.G. buys country house at Bellême, in Normandy.
1929	Starts work on *L'Appareillage*, original seventh volume of *Les Thibault*.
1930	Writes *Confidence Africaine*.
1931	Seriously injured in car-crash on New Year's Day; scraps original plan of *Les Thibault* and destroys *L'Appareillage*; writes *Un Taciturne* at Sauveterre, near Avignon.
1932	Writes *Vieille France* at Sauveterre.
1933	Draws up new plan for conclusion of *Les Thibault* and begins documentation for *L'Eté 1914*.
1934	Moves to Nice.
1936	Concludes *L'Eté 1914*.
1937	At Bellême, working on *Epilogue*; awarded Nobel Prize.
1939	Completes *Epilogue*.
1940–4	Spends most of Occupation in Nice.
1941	Begins *Le Journal du Colonel Maumort*.
1949	Death of wife at Nice.

1951	Witnesses death of Gide in Paris.
1954	Health begins to deteriorate.
1957	Prepares his archives for posthumous publication; deposits *Journal* in Bibliothèque Nationale.
1958	Hands over to Jean Delay his correspondence with Gide and Copeau; dies suddenly after heart-attack, 22 August, at Bellême.

Bibliography

(Place of publication, Paris, unless otherwise stated)

(A) WORKS OF MARTIN DU GARD

1909 *L'Abbaye de Jumièges* (archaeological thesis); *Grou-Radenz,* Montdidier; *Devenir!* Ollendorff.

1910 *L'une de nous . . .*, Grasset.

1913 *Jean Barois*, Gallimard.

1920 *Le Testament du Père Leleu*, Gallimard.

1921 *Témoignage* (tribute to l'Abbé Hébert), Grou-Radenz.

1922 *Le Cahier gris* (first part of *Les Thibault*), Gallimard.

Le Pénitencier (second part of *Les Thibault*), Gallimard.

1923 *La Belle Saison*, two volumes (third part of *Les Thibault*), Gallimard.

1928 *Noizemont-les-Vierges*, A la Lampe d'Aladdin, Liège.

La Gonfle, Gallimard.

La Consultation (fourth part of *Les Thibault*), Gallimard.

La Sorellina (fifth part of *Les Thibault*), Gallimard.

1929 *La Mort du Père* (sixth part of *Les Thibault*), Gallimard.

1930 *Dialogue*, Claude Aveline.

1931 *Confidence Africaine*, Gallimard.

1933 *Un Taciturne*, Gallimard.
Vieille France, Gallimard.

1936 *L'Eté 1914*, three volumes (seventh part of *Les Thibault*), Gallimard.

1940 *Epilogue* (last part of *Les Thibault*), Gallimard.

1951 *Notes sur André Gide*, Gallimard.

1955 *Oeuvres Complètes*, two volumes, including *Souvenirs Autobiographiques et Littéraires* ("Bibliothèque de la Pléiade"), Gallimard. Referred to in the text as *O.C.*

(B) ENGLISH TRANSLATIONS OF MARTIN DU GARD'S WORKS

1939 *The World of the Thibaults* (Parts 1–6), trans. Stuart Gilbert, John Lane, London.

1940 *Summer 1914* (Parts 7–8), trans. *idem*, John Lane, London.

1950 *Jean Barois*, trans. *idem*, John Lane.

1953 *Notes on André Gide*, trans. John Russell, André Deutsch.

1954 *The Postman* (*Vieille France*), trans. *idem*, André Deutsch.

(C) BOOKS OR ARTICLES ON MARTIN DU GARD

Borgal, C.: *Roger Martin du Gard* ("Classiques du XXe Siècle"), Editions universitaires, 1957.

Brenner, J.: *Martin du Gard*, Gallimard, 1961, (contains very full bibliography).

Camus, A.: Préface to Pléiade edition of *Oeuvres Complètes de Roger Martin du Gard*, Gallimard, 1955.

Gide, A.: *Journal 1889–1939*, Gallimard, 1939. (Various refs.)

Lalou, R.: *Roger Martin du Gard*, Gallimard, 1937.

Magny, C. E.: *Histoire du Roman Français depuis 1918*, Vol. I, Editions du Seuil, 1950, pp. 314 ff.

Nouvelle Revue Française: "Hommage à Roger Martin du Gard", December 1958.

Picon, G.: "Roger Martin du Gard"; article in *Mercure de France*, September 1958, pp. 5–25.

Prévost, J.: *Problèmes du Roman, Confluences*, Lyons and Paris, 1943. (Several refs.)

Rice, H. C.: *Roger Martin du Gard and the World of the Thibaults*, Viking Press, New York, 1941.

Wood, J. S.: "Roger Martin du Gard"; article in *French Studies*, April 1960.